CW00421190

Contents

Intro

I have had an idea. For my own sanity I am going to write about the daily minute emotions and events since the covid- 19 outbreak.

This is basically a diary of how I lost it and survived one of the most stressful times of our generation. It sounds dramatic, I know, and it was, at the time. Reading it all back now, it was a gift, in my circumstance anyway. Not for everyone.

There was a lot of things that went wrong, so many bright memories and a million other ways things could have gone.

This is my journey where some of the best memories of my life were made and where my inner most darkest fears conspired. Fear took over my life and left a shell of what I once was. However, this just gave space for a new projects. How did any of us survive?

I'm not sure, but it has been one heck of a ride.

Not everything here may be 100 percent fact, but it is as close to the mark as to what I believed at that given time. It is not all bad and it's not all good, and in the end, we are definitely not the same. I try my best not to give names of people or places because really, these special things just are not for sharing. If you find some bit rather vague, its for a reason. I am either protecting someone else or myself from any more heartbreak. I just cannot be that much of a knob.

This also contains loads of profanities, slang and made-up words. Just because. None of this is jointed and is a free-flowing blurb of my thoughts in the exact order they fall out of my head.

Not everything will make sense I imagine but if one thing does then surely that counts as success. Either way, it is always something to read on the loo.
I blabber on enough in this book for any further introductions.
Good Lu

Corona time

This all kicked off in December, not that many of us knew about it at first. Originated in China through some guy eating a bat or something to that effect or another secret government assault that infected a shed load of people, probably something to do with America, as it always is.

China kind of got a foot up their arse and dealt with it and are now almost on the other side. We watched the news and thought "jeez oh" I'm glad that's not here. Then rather quickly borders were not shut, people were flying all over the place and spread the virus like fire.

At that point we were still going about our daily lives and going to work having a bit of a laugh and joke (nothing too crude) until I got a text from a friend who had been in Italy saying that she was quarantined at home and her partner was in hospital with the virus. This friend lived in the next town to ours (joined by a bridge) and it freaked me out how close to home it was. I appealed to my bosses who in essence were in denial and confused, as although they were my bosses and my bosses boss, they still weren't allowed to make a decision on their own.
Common sense was not allowed.

Things started to gear up as more cases were confirmed in the UK, however reminding people to wash their hands whilst singing happy birthday wasn't much of a deterrent. Cross contamination gave me multiple panic attacks through the start of march, although still not enough to make me refuse to go to work. School closures were being brought up and as the week started, I began thinking what the heck? Why aren't we reacting to this? Still not enough to not send my children to nursery/playgroup.

I was unintentionally throwing common sense to the wind and putting my trust in our government, who I thought obviously knew more than me. They weren't panicking. Why should I?

Fast forward a few days, to the second last day of school. A discussion in the playground with 2 other mums. We agreed it was all our fault. I had personally asked, to anyone who was listening, for a break. I wanted more time to spend with my kids, quality time to love them for who they are and to leave normal life for a while.

Multiple things had happened in the past 2 years within my relationship, with my kids, with my family and with work that I had decided I wanted a break from it all. Before my friend told me about her having coronavirus a large argument had ensued with my partner and it tipped me over the edge. I wanted it to all be over and for a break to reveal a happier life or at least less hurt and pain.

The other mum mentioned she didn't want her neighbours to move and had asked the gods of the world for assistance... hence why she thought this could be her fault. Problem solved neighbours can't move. So, apologies in advance it was us.

The following day the schools closed, and we said goodbyes to my eldest son's nursery teachers, all eyes filled with tears. The head nursery teacher said hello, I returned a quick "hi" before turning my head away in fear of bawling my eyes out about how devastated I was. This was probably going to be my eldest's last day as a proper young child. He would be in primary one after the summer. One new main teacher and a whole different ball game.

The nursery teachers had been the most caring and loving individuals you could imagine. Doing everything you could want for my child. Supporting him in his times of need, encouraging him at his strengths and judging by the tears and eyes full of sorrow and fear, loving my boy as much as I loved him. For this I am eternally grateful.

How to explain this situation to a 4 year old. I genuinely had no idea, they however did a pretty good job of this too, explaining germs and why it is important to wash our hands giving me a new excuse to why everything around his normal life was closing. "It's the bugs" and he would take this as a solid explanation.

As a final farewell to my youngest son's friends, we had a playdate in the morning discussing how terrified we were and how much we would miss moaning to each other about our lives. Would this be the toughest aspect of our life? Possibly. Yet to confirm this, however I do miss my moaning friends a lot.

I also miss the people we accidentally see on a regular basis, the bin lady who we talk to at least once a day on the school run, the receptionists at my work (also where my sons playgroup is) asking how we are, charming the attitude and daily musings out of us and my very close friend (who was also a receptionist) joining us for swimming, visiting the house for a news and to chill, buying pancakes and surprising me for breakfast at work. All these small things and so many more we would miss for who knows how long.

The unknown is terrifying.

The day the schools closed was also the day my work closed to the public. We carried out our regular duties and gave the last group of classes their final swimming lessons for a while, wondering if they would still be able to swim by the time they came back. We did a few things that would not usually be done in lessons and pushed some boundaries as the maximum we had in our classes combined was 4.

Evidently parents were being very clever and kept their kids at home long before they were being told to.

It was a solemn feeling leaving work that night wondering when we would greet the public through the doors again.

I however still had to go into work to clean the building for the foreseeable (turned out to be 2 shifts) to which I looked forward to really, as it would be a relaxed version of what I usually get paid to do. Team bonding began and we had a great couple of shifts before leaving the building with the prospect of being used elsewhere within the community.

Day 1 was a Saturday so in essence should have been like any other, however this was not true. As it turns out, being totally terrified 90% of the time and being dismissed by others who don't see the issues as fearfully as you do is exhausting! And on this day one of my biggest decisions was whether or not to wear my fit bit as I probably wouldn't achieve my desired 10,000 steps in a day.

This quickly changed as my desire to do anything did also. I wanted to sleep, and my body decided it needed to sleep too. I slept for the majority of the day on Saturday and Sunday and when I wasn't sleeping, I was creating an argument or being the most impatient human to have graced the earth. I didn't like myself and more importantly didn't like what I was doing to my family. I gave into the exhaustion and slept as much as I could feeling as if the events from 2 years' worth of shit was finally catching up and needed to be dreamt away.

It was very common before the outbreak began for me to have nightmares, mostly irrational and fear based, most of them scorched into my brain however I had one in around November time which was almost like a fleeting thought that turned to obsession. It was about all of the things that could harm my children in the world that I could do nothing about.

In this instance it was a virus. I couldn't protect my kids from what I could not see, and this caused a lot of tension and worry, however I had no way to deal with this and it would be a "take it as it comes" scenario. How naive.

I usually rationalised everything as much as possible and prepared anything that may be of use in the situation, this usually relieved the feelings of panic and helplessness. For example, a year ago after rescuing someone from the pool with a colleague I forgot to catch the gentleman's head as we lifted him out of the water, however my colleague remembered to do this crucial thing, hence why the casualty was ok in real life. The situation was dealt with amazingly and the teamwork was on par.

This materialised in a dream as my family in a car accident in a canal, the car turned on its side and my partner in the back with the children. We had already been in a car accident before, so I knew his quick thinking, so as we were crashing, he was unbuckling the kids to get them out. I managed to get out of my seat and into the back (God knows how as it's only a fiesta) winding down the window as far as it would go, ready to retrieve the kids. I got out and took my youngest child to the surface, guiding him to some rusty ladders to climb. Within seconds I retrieved my eldest child from the car and got him to the ladders. However, the dream quickly ended here the first time as my youngest wandered onto the road in the dark and would be killed. This couldn't be done.

Second, returning to the dream, as we get to the ladders, I climb up also and instruct my eldest to get his brother and pin him down without hurting him, and do whatever he needs to do to keep him safe. This scenario worked so the dream continued. No sign of my partner coming up from the water. I dive back in and find him wedged in the window, unable to get out. I try pulling, breaking the window, whatever I can but it won't work. He dies.

Ok so re-run through the whole dream again I get to this point to help my partner, I remember a device I kept on my key chain to break windows and cut seat belts (bought after another creepy nightmare a year or so earlier) so I get it and break the window. I pull him to the surface and carry him over my shoulder to the top with this glistening shine of light that everything will be ok. We get to the top and I lay him down on the gravel, kids looking over him, but what do I forget? I didn't catch his head. It thumps on the ground and blood comes pouring out. He's dead. Again. Shit.

No matter how many times I replay this dream I cannot change the final outcome. He always dies. So, I began to realise that this had come from the incident at the pool. I hadn't caught the gentleman's head and so without help he wouldn't have been ok mirroring exactly everything in my dream. Well at least this is what I think it meant either that or I'm bat shit crazy, both of which could be rather believable.

Ok, so that got a bit deep and crazy there quickly, however my point was that I had already had this fear and nightmare however didn't actually find a coping mechanism that would prepare me in real life and now it was real life. No wonder I slept for a weekend.

Anyway, Monday arrived, and I got to see my nervous work friends and boss before the building was officially shut to staff. Lockdown was about to begin anytime now, and I was not prepared. Well, I was minimally prepared. Everyone was panic buying shit paper and beans, and I was panic buying a bike for my son's 5th birthday the following month. Turned out to be a pretty good idea as all the Argos shut within a few days of my purchase. I felt like I was winning at life and nailing the pandemic, even though I would have to keep a bike in my bedroom cupboard for weeks tenderly having to open the door in case it squashed me.

This feeling faded quickly as I also began to wonder what would happen to my family. Ahh shit, back to having no control again. I have a few main concerns:

my grandparents- I had already phoned and told I would not be up to see them for the foreseeable, if they need anything at all I can be the delivery driver!

My dad- we discussed how he should look after himself and he explained, I've been through a lot worse, look what I've battled in my lifetime, I'll be fine and if I'm not I love you all to bits and I'm very proud of you all.

My sister and nephews- bad asthma with their own business and a loving husband who was already taking care of everything.

My mum is self-isolating at home on her own. Says she's fine as she doesn't have a fever but has every other symptom.

Multiple friends with children and kids. Most of whom have partners working offshore or are at risk due to previous medical conditions.

Friends who live so far away with kids but who are seriously loved by their own support networks.

Friends who live close with no kids but many vulnerable people and situations around them.

My friend who I hugged goodbye as we left our last shift because I told her I already missed her hugs, who might also be already infected as she was at the last massive concert in Scotland before lockdown.

The ones who don't have friends, family and others to help, or the resources to feed themselves or kids or enough money to pay rent and bills.

Those who are grieving loved ones just past. Those who have just brought new life to this scary as fuck world.

There's too much to be fearful of. Everyone's life is on hold, and I have no idea how to remove the sinking feeling of being stuck in quicksand waiting for the world to eat us all up.

We need to try and get by and take this as a blessing of time, even though loads of people will die, and it seems to be random selection at this time.

Current methods include focussing on improving the playgroup. As a member of the amazing committee, I can help this group succeed when we can return to life as we previously knew it. Also watching every movie, I watched as a child to pass on the wisdom of Thumbelina and grease. We watched Transformers "to learn about robotics". Win win.

Sinking ships

Day 5 and new coping methods include trying to home-school a 4-year-old and a 2 year old. This was hard and we tried to be teachers, forgetting that kids at this age tend to learn through play rather than sitting still and listening.

Wish this had dawned on me at the start of the day rather than the end. Change of plan, a long walk in the woods, climbing trees and avoiding people.

My partner and I seem to have this unspoken agreement about arguments at this time. We know life is a stressful situation, therefore an argument isn't taken personally, and as soon as there is a silence between us for about 3 seconds, which counts as the issue being resolved. It's a win win for the time being. The kids on the other hand don't have a filter and I think they already have had enough time at home, so the whining and crying is a lot, however they are punching each other a little less than normal.
Silver linings and all that.

Tomorrow will be different, or not. Either way it's another day I get to spend on this earth and think about all the other souls dealing with the same shit as I am. Shit mams crew as my friend likes to call it!

Loose wires

So, at this moment in time life should be about making the most of the time with the children. Teaching them anything and everything using Pinterest as my source of imagination, since unfortunately I have lost my own and inventing new things to do now evades me.

All this said, I cannot seem to connect myself to my brain. I feel my body working and going through the motions but not physically connecting to the world around me. However, because I recognize this, I can act and make a change. For example, today I signed up for Disney+. The saviour of the pandemic for many and hopefully the saviour of my sanity.

Okay, 1 movie in and my mood and attitude has lifted amazingly. Who knew that the source of happiness is actually animation and catchy tunes?

When life gives you lemons, you're supposed to make lemonade. That was today. Early morning and waking up with the focus of no pressure. No pressure to perform like a teacher, no pressure to be the best mum in the world, no pressure to go to work, no pressure to do anything.

This mindset worked for today. Had some breakfast and watched a movie. Set up our itinerary for the day, playdough, gymnastics, football, music and numbers. All apart from gymnastics were achieved, however we did so much more not relying on having to fix our lives. We made pancakes, went on a big bike run, juggled with tangerines, played in the garden, drew rainbows and a lion on our windows, drew pictures, face painting, updated nursery teachers on the daily musings, completed work sent by my boss and a million other moments in between.

The lion on our window was the last thing we did before going to bed. To my kids it was a trigger to see if it would make any passers-by smile. To me it symbolised so much of the world and our personal battles. The lion represents us all in our current state.

We fight for survival or what we genuinely think is survival in a first world country.

In essence we do not know what a hard life really is. The lion is all of the workers and NHS staff (who are absolute heroes) facing their own daily battles avoiding this horrible virus. The heart and soul of our country, hidden in plain sight for years.

A few years ago, I chose between 2 careers. Training to become a nurse or being a leisure attendant and basically a hyped up cleaner. At this point in time, I am glad I chose the latter. I choose an easy life. One that would promote fitness and job security whilst also being able to see my kids at work and it wouldn't particularly become life or death if I wasn't there. A job that requires me to be at home when there is a pandemic.

How did it take me days and days to realise this?

I am so lucky I don't have to panic about bringing this or any other viruses home to my family on a daily basis. When my kids get sick, I will care for them because there are people out there who are willing to care for others.

I feel it was a selfish choice. One I made so I could satisfy my immediate and irrational fears rather than using my brain for good.

I had never thought about being a nurse until I had my youngest child. From day 1 we spent a lot of time in hospital due to a magnitude of things, initially being polycythaemia which we sort of managed, then viral meningitis which led to sepsis. Another hurdle that we nailed, then liver disease and then ridiculous reflux, and the clincher was an unknown something that made his head swell and caused his body to retain too much fluid. To this day I have no idea what caused our final hospitalisation however all of this happened within the space of 6 months, and I wonder why I have a clingy child.

I don't really need to wonder about this anymore. I know why he is glued to me like a fly on shit, because all I did for 6 months was live, sleep, breathe and worry about this new baby we had brought into all of this trauma. I think when you spend so much time in the same place in a state of stress it becomes familiar and a sort of safe zone to an extent. The hospital is where all of this trauma was, however, it was also where it was mostly taken away.

Up until his first birthday I was grateful for many things involving the hospital.

One, for giving me the extra one-to-one time with my new-born child and two for highlighting all the support and love we had surrounding us and working to make my son better. We had people from all across the world praying to make my son better, family members who were as worried as I was, so much so they told their parish churches who told other parishes and they all prayed for my little boy.

I have no idea if this made a difference to his physical health, but it certainly made a difference to my mental health and filled me and the kind nurses who helped us with hope.

Whilst in hospital for the 3rd time I began feeling desperate and full of despair due to a multitude of things going on around us and the fact that we were stuck away from my eldest son AGAIN! I met this woman who asked us about our situation whilst trawling the halls with her own 6 month old child. I blurted everything out and explained how desperate I was for things to be alright. I then asked how she was doing.

This is when reality hit me like a brick, in fact less of a brick more of a big ass building coming down on top of me. Here I was moaning about my slightly ill child who had been through a lot, and she mentions that she was waiting to get blood results back for her daughter to see if they could get home 1 hour and a half hours away from her 3 other children. I think ok, nothing too much, maybe a virus or something. I enquired further as to what the results were for and as casual as ever the mum says "we need to see if her infection markers are low enough to spend 3 days at home before returning to start chemotherapy".
Her daughter had stage 4 liver cancer.

Boom.
Life comes tumbling down and I suddenly am so appreciative of the position I am in compared to her. 6 months old with a minimal survival rate. My bitching and moaning seem pathetic. I cried for her and had to stop myself as she tried to comfort me.

This mum did not need my tears and sorrow for her situation, she already knew the shit show she had been dealt. Whenever I catch myself complaining about the little things in this great life we have, I remember her and the strength that mum showed in the face of such adversity.
It was the source of all my fears, but this was her reality.

This would be the deciding factor for me. I spoke to a lovely nurse whose name evades me at this moment, however, was very kind and a genuinely extra mile type person. I asked if it was common to have babies with cancer. She replied that most of the people she treated on a daily basis were cancer kids. My face sank.

She loved her job and said it was the most rewarding work in the world, however the expectation is that any one of the kids she treats and gets to know, and love could die at any given time. Before her shift finished, we had a chuckle to lighten our mood and she smiled before saying "this one is going to be trouble" pointing at my innocently sleeping child. She was right, for a million different reasons.

I believe a lot in "life never gives us more than we can handle".
I realise now, I mostly believe this to boost my own ego. Thinking this way tends to give me the inner strength to never give up.

I certainly haven't been dealt the worst deal in the world, by a mile. However, I am pretty sick of the shit. I'm ready to attract all things of happiness and light.
This used to be what my life was like, and this was probably due to my attitude of finding the good in every situation. I mean, I have a tattoo of the African symbol for "hakuna matata" on my foot for fucks sake. You would think I could be a bit more chilled out.

For now, I'm trying and feel like I keep getting the effort kicked out of me, instead the empty space fills with fear and frustration.

This is until it all dissipates. Gone in wind once again, moved by a smile or a moment of peace. I don't mean peace and quiet like bliss but finding a moment of peace amongst the chaos of the world spiralling and children running around singing the most random songs. Usually, it's the music that brings me to peace. When your 2 year old starts singing some Dermot Kennedy, or my 4 year old recites word perfect the full song of "Donald where's your troosers"

It's maybe better described as being content.

Things that can make your life a little bit brighter is definitely a pet. For me the main ones are a cat and a dog. I have one of each, however I am most avidly a cat person, probably destined to live alone surrounded by 20 felines in my later life. Doesn't sound too shabby to me to be honest. However, because I have one of each and am this horrendous worrier, I must treat them both the same, ensuring they both get plenty of cuddle time and the love that they deserve. Heaven, forbid I forget to give equal cuddles and one feels left out or unloved.

Pets can give you similar feelings to that of a child. You get the love and loyalty, you get the responsibility and sorrow of when they leave this earthly plain. In essence they are amazing companions for our mental health and can reduce the feeling of loneliness.

In this situation loneliness is the by-product of the pandemic. It can be so easily conquered and yet is sometimes so hard to get passed. I saw my sister, her husband and my 3 beautiful nephews today. We were inside our house hanging out the front window and she was on the other side of our front garden wall. It wasn't much but it was familiar and a bright spot in this web of despair. There's nothing like seeing and hearing those who you love so dearly and can't even embrace or give a quick cuddle for fear of killing them by accident.

So, they say absence makes the heart grow fonder. I'm assuming this is for all relationships as when I see my friends it makes me love them even more, especially when it is a brief visit at a 3 metres minimum distance.

We attempted to walk the dog this morning, to try and wake ourselves up. We made it 10 metres from the garden before turning back. Another stupid irrational fear had kicked in and the thought of how much the kids would touch and how I didn't have enough hands to protect them from the world whilst holding the dog. 10 metres and my heart was pounding out of my chest. Feeling ready to vomit and head spinning with fear, guilt, love and panic. Fuck it. It's really not worth it right now. New motto "pick your battles".

This absolute pile of nonsense stemmed from my lovely isolated mum sending some really interesting videos of a mole who had been busy in her garden. You could physically see the little guy moving the dirt just below the surface.

We were messaging back and forth in a family group chat having a laugh and I happened to say "I was waiting for you to bop him on the head" as in whack a mole little bunny foo foo style. My sister joined in, and we laughed a lot, well I certainly did.

At this point I headed downstairs to let my dog into the back garden, opening the door ushering him out. I saw this strange thing on the grass. It's a little mole lying belly up, paws in the air, definitely dead pose.

I mean what the fuck. What is the great earthly meaning to this, do I need to do some soul searching?

I made one silly joke about killing a mole and the world presents me with one at my door. Maybe I should start making jokes about treasure chests full of cash and chocolate, see what lands on my door.

Anyway, fast forward past the failed walk, we are playing football in the garden and a friend walks past with her 2 kids the same ages as mine. It's like seeing sunshine in the morning.

We talk for about 20 minutes across the wall trying to keep the kids from touching or getting too close. I tell her about this little mole and the significance and she's as freaked as me.

However, as she is having a good day due to the fact that the sun is out and she believes she is solar powered, she brings me out of defcon 1. "I wouldn't read too much into it, it's a beautiful day" and just like that, panic is gone.

So, our day was turned around with a few words, and because of this we decided to do a few things for others. We make a delivery of food to my grandparents, and we deliver some chocolate to other mums who I know are worried about life right now and one of my oldest son's friends. They are all so delighted and grateful, however the best part about this was getting my son to deliver these parcels to the door, knock and run away.

He sat waiting in the car for them all to open the door and the sheer excitement and happiness when they emerged confused and then extremely happy. Best home-school lesson ever.

The day continued this way and in essence we did some gardening, played hopscotch and went worm hunting. Some seriously delighted kids and one happy mum.

I'm pretty sure this was because, even though it was brief, I saw some of my favourite people today from a distance and that was enough. Enough to change fear to calm and enough to save my sanity for another day.

For today, I am grateful. It's only taken me a week of isolation, but for today everything was beautiful and funny. The eerie silence at night after bedtime wasn't scary; it was bliss.

Instead of a moment of peace in chaos, every moment was content.

Don't get me wrong I still had to give my kids into trouble for misbehaving, however rather than feeling the burning sensation in my chest, it was a quiet telling off that disappeared almost immediately after. We relaxed and enjoyed each other's company, revelled in silly jokes and behaviour and watched Disney. Again.

One thing that I did today differently was receive hope. Whilst out in the garden a woman and her son walked past with their dog. I see this woman often and we chat and have a general laugh about life.

Today we spoke about a challenge we both face in life called alopecia. She lost around 80 percent of her hair a few years ago. It got to the point where she asked her partner to shave the whole lot off. She also explained about using light therapy. Basically, going to Aberdeen twice a week to chill in a sunbed. Her funny anecdotal way of reciting how she made lemonade with her situation and stripped during her light therapy and got a free tan. As an added bonus, her hair grew back beautifully.

I mentioned that I had been dying to shave my hair off for months, and she highlighted, what better time to do it?

Now I know how this sounds, I already seem bat shit crazy. If I was to go full Britney, I'm sure they would carry me off to some hospital, and we all know that is not the place to be at this point.

Still not set on the idea as my urge to be bald has lessened since not brushing my hair for a week because I won't really be seen in public. When the apocalypse is over the idea might resurface.

We have made it a week with no school, and day 5 of lockdown. Word is that the measures are about to get stricter as people cannot stay away from each other, either because they won't be told what to do, or they really do not like who they live with.

Panic arrived this morning. I'll maybe rename it, because even the word makes the feeling more intense. I think we shall call it daisy. Maybe.

Anyway, it was there when I woke up and I know exactly why. My partner developed a bit of a sore throat at work yesterday, he was breathless and generally feeling awful. Daisy appeared because I worried, he wasn't ok. I worried about who he had infected at work and home. I worried about not being able to get dog food or supply my grandparents with meat they asked for or the weekly shop my mum had asked for.

Daisy hung around for most of the day mixing with tiredness and frustration. However, we still had a lazy Saturday. Mulled around playing games and watching movies and a nice wander to the woods which has grown ever busy since lockdown.
The weather was windy and cold today with a shower of hail so there were less people around. Barely anyone walked past the house which has been like a main street the past few days because the sun was out.

I wouldn't call the day lonely in fact far from it, but life felt more disconnected. Less strangers to watch and less desire to go out into the world. I did however connect with a few random moments today; a bubble that drifted through the air after putting fairy liquid into my sink. It was small and pretty. It brought a smile to my face which grew even more with the thought of me grinning at a bubble.

We watched a toy story today and my eldest son, who I thought was rather bored, was far from it. He was so engrossed in the movie that he celebrated for Woody succeeding at the end of the movie. I'd love to say which part, but I was distracted by a silly game on my phone, something I never get to usually do because it feels like I'm wasting time.
His joyful face for a fictional character made my heart smile and released a desire to be involved in his happiness.

The desire to do anything is a lot. This whole situation is a lot but really on the grand scale of things its normal daily life for others. Not the whole living with a deadly virus part but living in fear and in worse conditions than what we are in just now means I am still very grateful. I have a home, a partner who adores our amazing children, 2 cracking pets and a large circle of people who I care about and who in turn cares about us.

The circle is larger than I imagined and becomes highlighted in these circumstances. The circle also helps keep Daisy at bay. My dad video called me tonight and it was so nice to see his face. It was gutting to see him under so much pressure from still working and trying to make sure he looked after his employees, but hearing his voice was a treat.

Another little treat today was feeling like I had achieved something. I found an app that I could download that helps teach kids about words and sounds.

Letters don't usually interest my eldest, but this game was a hit and he definitely learned from it. He loves video games so I'm thinking if he's playing this all day long then at least he's building a positive relationship with learning.

Also, my patience doesn't get pounded because I like the game too and usually the whole look and listen to me idea does not happen. At the same time, I was able to build a puzzle with my youngest. Most content part of the day.

April 2020

I haven't written since the 28th of march. This is now the 1st of April which is a triumph as march seemed to be the longest month ever. Worse than January. 2020 has been a year of saying "really?" the whole thing has needed to be reset and that's pretty much from the 1st.

I haven't had the energy to write or even use my brain for more than the basic necessities. I was at Tesco the other day and it was terrifying. Literally the most on edge I've felt. We queued outside the shop 2 metres apart and were let in intermittently. I had to do the shop as I am the only driver in the house.

As I got into the shop, I wandered round picking up what I needed, keeping my distance from others. Not that everyone followed these rules. Luckily the small town I live in has the most amazing staff who were more than helpful as I tried keeping my heart rate to a minimum. I was out quickly and had to go to 2 more shops to get everything we required.

As I headed home after dropping what my mum needed, I realised this whole ordeal had taken 2 hours. 2 hours of my life consumed by the world and all its deepening darkness. I was more than grateful to reach the safety of my home. Of course, I then proceeded to drop a dozen eggs across my car and the ground, guess who's not having eggs for the next week.

The rest of the Sunday was good, but I couldn't tell if I was just stressed or feeling unwell. Turns out I was feeling ill. My throat began to ache, and my body couldn't keep up with the energy my brain had, and that wasn't much either.

Monday came and my partner had to go back to work. He felt fine and I got to deal with life at home with nothing left in the barrel. It was fine, we survived, mainly because my kids have a good routine and can understand being ill. They know how to make you feel better including loads of cuddles and entertaining themselves. For my children I am so grateful.

We did printed worksheets that they loved and repainted our front window with a sunshine theme. We even did some gardening that was brought to halt due to shitty weather of course, but another Disney movie to rescue.

We video called some friends, my sister and the kids' grandparents. The video call with my sister and her 3 boys mostly included farts and nakedness but was exactly as expected, total chaos and happiness. I love the isolation with these two beautiful souls and seeing our family reminds us of why we do so. My partner texted and phoned as often as he could to keep a check on us and to make sure we were coping, he wasn't completely throwing us under the bus. I appreciate the affection even when it comes in strange forms.

I got an update from a few of my eldest's teachers about ideas of what to do and how they were coping with isolation. Friendly faces who have given my child so much, who I'm not sure we will have many dealing with in the future unfortunately. For them, I am also grateful.

Our postman knocked on our window to give us a thumbs up for our new design on the window and another friend messaged to say how her partner who never usually would notice things like that came home and told how it had cheered him up.

The power and influence we have inside of our homes are not something that is usually recognised. We feel minute and unable to contribute to the bigger picture doing nothing at home, when in essence we can do so much. The world will not and should not be the same after this pandemic.

Ideally life will flourish and grow. Our families will be grateful and full of love rather than loathing. Our mind full of boredom could create the unknown.
I believe having the time to be bored is the source of many great ideas. It is also how people build their mental strength. Having the time and space to count an amount of floor tiles or to doodle on a piece of paper creates sparks in imagination and confidence.

Being confined to our home and just having my kids as a focal point makes me feel like the world's best mum. My kids are confident in their skills because they have no one to compare themselves to. I have no one to compare myself to. I could if I really wanted to, but seeing other parents or practitioners post on social media gives me ideas on what to do, as long as I have the energy to follow it through.

I love to see parts of people I never usually would, and I can sit here cheering them on, being proud of who they are in their own right. I now fear the end of lockdown where I have to return to the craziness that is life. The pressure and need to keep moving forward. Next mission is finding a way to integrate this standstill type of living into work life.

We saw my mother in law today also from the other side of the garden wall. She was delighted and so were the kids. She is still working as a carer at 2 jobs and hasn't had a day off for a few weeks now. We don't hear much from her just now unfortunately because she is still working. The bonus is that the kids spoke so much as they didn't take her time for granted. They shouted love you a million times until she got into her car as they had missed her so much.

One of the funniest moments we've had today has been at supper time. My youngest doesn't do well with cold at all.
"I Don't like ice cream or the rain because it's all so cold".
He wanted an ice pole for pudding to which I obliged. After about 3 minutes of screwed up faces and nibbling he asked me to blow his ice pole because it was too cold. Cue him putting the stick in his mouth and trying to blow as you would through a straw. My eldest and I both had a laugh and this innocent 2 year old carries on until he is satisfied with the temperature. I was waiting for the suggestion of it being put in the microwave, having flashes of his horrified face as I pulled out juice and a stick. Luckily it didn't come to that.

We watched The Good Dinosaur tonight and became completely absorbed in the underrated movie. Both of the kids were excited for him to the point of almost crying. The sadness in his eyes (spoiler alert) as his dad was swept away and the hopefulness as they kept saying "he needs to get home to his mummy". I felt like the most loved mum in the world surrounded by my boys, one of whom kept climbing into my arms to tell me that he loved me. In the movie one of the dinosaurs says "if you aren't scared, you aren't alive"
Obviously living my life as a paranoid fearmonger this resonated with me and made me feel human. I know it's sad, but kids ' movies make me emotional and I don't care. I cried at Cars 3 the other day as Lightning McQueen crashed himself in slow motion. It's hard to watch.

My son watched me cry today, happy tears of course at the dinosaur movie and as he looked at me his face became sad. I found myself reminding him with a smile on my face that it is more than ok to cry, especially when you're happy. Tears are not something to be afraid of.

What also strikes me as odd, and I don't know if I'm the only one who notices this, but when people shake hands in a movie or if they touch something like a door handle a thought comes striking through my head "he shouldn't be doing that, he needs to wash his hand".
 It must not take a lot to brainwash me as a week and a half into lockdown and I am already preconditioned to immaculate hand hygiene and where it is easy to catch germs from. What is this going to look like on the other side?

With my extra time I have been using it wisely, doing important stuff, which I say sarcastically as I cleaned my oven and resealed my bath. They were jobs that needed done but really, I probably could have been a bit more useful elsewhere.

Simple pleasures

So last night my eldest woke up early doors feeling ill, that's both of the kids now feeling the effects of whatever bug we have, be it the flu or this awful virus. However, we still managed to muster the energy to colour in a multitude of pictures and "school work". I found myself wondering how much harder this would be without the entertainment of having kids and a partner to amuse. I can only imagine the quiet and peace that they live in every day.

Silence must be golden.

Also, the idea of shaving my head returned the past few days and I was trying to think of a million other ways to conquer the annoyance. I have had alopecia since I was 16 but never quite as bad that it took over my life. I tried to use the knowledge I had built up about herbs and natural remedies to create a magical concoction that would somehow make my hair grow.

Okay I'll admit, I did this a few days ago and can only just now write about it, because I did a few hair related things.

So, after making this magical juice of turmeric and a few other things, I smothered my hair in it and wrapped and cling film, with a cosy hat on top for good measure. After leaving it for a couple of hours I washed it out and noticed the overwhelming smell of turmeric, even after a double shampoo. 5 days later and I'm still smelling it. Oops.

After the smell had kind of died down a little, I proceeded to put something spicy on my bald patches in an effort to stimulate growth. The spiciest thing I had in my house at this point was reggae reggae medium sauce and like the absolute tool I am, smothered the patches in this tasty brown stuff until I could feel it burning.

At which point I washed it off before I went on fire and before it got too painful, because I am a massive wimp. I smell like the dodgiest curry you've ever seen but I feel like I have made progress or at least an effort. Oh, and if that wasn't enough, I gave myself the first quarantine haircut and chopped about 3 inches off all round. Good job, I won't be seeing anyone for a while. Starting to think going bald would have been easier.

Daisy hasn't been extremely prevalent in my day today which has been overwhelmingly lovely.

I've eased myself into the madness and am enjoying having a chance to draw and write. Mostly sonic and SpongeBob but it all counts.

The simple pleasures in life seem to be what encourages natural happiness. My partner and I demonstrated the moves to "kung fu fighting" whilst my kids were finishing their supper, actually being gentle with each other and laughing at ourselves for a change. We are still sitting in opposite rooms doing our own thing just now as the kids sleep but I know today I have been able to smile, laugh and be silly like I haven't been for a long time.

I also had a zoom call with 2 of my sisters and mum which was brilliant. We laughed and had no stress just catching up as if the world had stopped. Which it pretty much has. Well for myself that is not a key worker. My mum is a key worker but has had to self-quarantine as she was ill and one of my sisters is also a key worker in a mental health unit, however, is pregnant and has been working from home for a month. We have all had some time to recuperate who we are. There's only so many days you can stay at a high level of stress without any immediate risk.

The risk we are facing is long and drawn out, with signs of it possibly lasting until July. That's 4 months. I'm not sure if we will bypass the happy stage and into insanity and who knows what my hair will look like.

Master of guilt

Early mornings are becoming a thing for us now and strangely for me they are becoming quite enjoyable. It's not like me to enjoy my mornings, but once again because of the lack of pressure to go anywhere, they are slow, calm and fun.

Also, an early morning cup of tea is something to look forward to and as soon as that cup is finished, I can have another, and another and another. By the end of this I may be drinking myself into a tea coma. Either way it's enjoyable.

Isolation changed today for me. I received a few phone calls from my boss about being re-deployed into a different industry.

Good news you may think, possibly. I'm not so sure. I had just adjusted to my life as a full time mum again and loved the prospect of getting up every day having nowhere to go, but having the time to create new adventures for my kids and now I'm going to have to throw myself into the working world again.

I am to be deployed in a school next week to help supervise and create activities for the kids of parents who are key workers. Usually, I would be excited about the whole prospect of it and having a new challenge to sink my teeth into, however I am already missing the time I get to spend with the kids, and I haven't even started yet.

I am also to report to a local care home to help with cleaning duties and basically fill in for members of staff who are off sick. Here I was thinking I had loads of talent and I could be learning new exciting skills, but not a glorified cleaner once again. I wouldn't exactly say no as I am currently being paid whilst I lounge around at home enjoying my life.

I am worried about the idea of having this virus and entering an environment with many others who are vulnerable with the possibility of killing them or bringing it home to my family and ruining their lives, but once again I am bound by the rules of a contract where I have to comply with what I am being told to do. My peace and comfort are about to be obliterated.

I feel like it's a step backwards from the job I left to become a leisure attendant, but in essence we all have to do our part to contribute. It doesn't make me any less gutted.

I was hoping out of all the 700 staff sitting in retention at home, I would be one of the lucky ones. How selfish I know, but my love and lustre to be there every day of my kids life ladens me with guilt.

Being a mum gives a whole new meaning to the word guilt. It exists in everyday life from the moment you are aware of their existence. I don't know if it's hormones or love, but it is overwhelming. The guilt I had when my eldest was born was daily. Every Time he cried, and I couldn't soothe him. When I would co-sleep with him I had fear and guilt. When I cooked something that wasn't super nutritious, when I dressed him in clothes rather than a onesie, when I tried to teach him to sleep in his own bed.

None of this compared to the guilt I felt when I fell pregnant with my youngest. The idea that I was no longer putting him first, that I couldn't run around as much as before, when I would have to leave him at home to be in labour. Then finally when he was born, I had to stay in hospital for 6 days without my eldest. His whole life was turned upside down and it was planned.

Things didn't get any easier from there either. The guilt piled on in a big way after the multiple trips and staying in the hospital looking after this new soul, not being able to support my eldest at home. This encapsulated the fear of losing my new-born and I'm not really surprised my brain had the reaction it did.

The whole situation was disjointed and confusing for me so for him it must have been a whirlwind of emotions. I know for a fact the day we went to hospital in the ambulance stuck in his mind and was traumatic for him. Everything was fun and fine and then next minute random strangers are in our house and his mum and brother are gone in a flashing big truck, who knows when to be seen again.

He is a very brave soul and is knowledgeable so when situations like this come up, he asks loads of questions to which we reply honestly. Well as appropriately honest for a 4 year old as can be.

My friend from work fell at home and knocked herself out in the middle of the night about a year ago. She was home alone with her 2 girls as her partner works offshore. She split her head and lay on the floor for a length of time before coming to. She awoke and had to call numerous people, one to take her to hospital and someone else to come and sit with her children.

Luckily, she was ok and had a large support network around her to help. When she got home, she taught her kids what to do in a situation like that where she was helpless. She wrote phone numbers down of people to call and made sure they knew what number to dial for help.

I did the same on a smaller scale as her kids are a few years older than mine and can read well. My eldest knows how to call the emergency services and he knows if he can't get through then he can go to one of our neighbours houses. However, he also has a much younger brother in tow to keep safe. This is the part I don't think about too often as there are numerous situations in which it could all go wrong, and they both end up hurt also.
For a while I wondered what would happen if I was to be hurt at home when it was just me and the kids. This is when I noticed how little people contact us and it's not a bad thing really as I am terrible at replying or remembering to check on people.

I get very lost in my own bubble of contentment away from the outside world. However, for the sake of my kids safety and for a million other reasons I have a network of people I can rely on and who I hope know, they can rely on me.

I've had to rewire my way of thinking and how much I enjoy isolation and the phrase "it takes a village to raise a family" brings a whole new meaning. I used to think this was all about who you let look after your kids and who they spend time with, but in essence it's who would be there for them at all times. For my friends and family, I am grateful.

The past few days we have done so much. We have finished weeding the garden (which I replanted weeds thinking they were strawberries), built a fire in the garden, found a centipede and a ladybird along with a million other beasties, drank copious amounts of tea, decorated our upstairs window with Olaf, began stupidly painting our garden fence with very watery paint, sent about 1 million videos to my eldest's girlfriend, had a massive bike ride, learned how to play kirby and had a video call from my dad.

All of which has been rather satisfying apart from the watery paint. The happiness of it all has made us more reclusive into our own family to the point where I barely touch my phone or message anyone because we are so busy. What a change from last week.

The days have blurred into one and I got the shock of my life when I realised it was Saturday again meaning that we had survived another week in lockdown. Without the boys I don't imagine time would pass so quickly. I haven't been watching the news or even keeping up to date online about covid-19 so when I checked today, and the UK death toll was now in the 4000 mark I got the shock of a lifetime.

It's serious and so many are dying from this one of whom was apparently a 5 year old boy. Today was not the day I should have checked for updates.

People still aren't taking it all too seriously and not being in public places keeps you out of the loop of this idea. Today we did have to go to "the big shop" for a few things and I was still surprised by how close people were happy to be to each other and how little disregard some had for staff in shops.

At one of our local shops, we now have to ask at the counter to receive toilet rolls in an attempt to preserve supplies for everyone. Is it not madness that we have to protect some people from their own stupidity? Andrex will certainly be making a mint from their sales right now however I do wonder where all the loo roll goes?

Many pictures race through my mind of people inhaling it and using it to sleep on but I'm pretty sure things haven't gotten that bad. Yet.

Ballsy

The weekend is over once again, and it passed without me even noticing. Apparently, people were out this weekend, where I have no idea. Everywhere is shut. Unless they are partying in a Tesco car park or something. Once again, the stupidity of a nation affects us all. On the bright side this won't end soon, and we can continue to get a break from the chaos.

I went to work on Monday for the first time in two weeks. This was my first redeployment into the local primary school. I thought that there wouldn't be a lot of children and in essence there were only 6. Still more than what I expected, which was nice and humbling.

Each one of their parents and carers were nurses. Essential work that needs to be carried out and cannot stop, the lifeline of the country.
I am there again tomorrow afternoon and I'm kind of looking forward to it. It's a strange feeling really because it's not excitement or actual joy about working, it's just meh. If meh were an actual proper description of a feeling.
I've heard a little bit about the care home I was supposed to be inducted in today and have currently refused to go until it is necessary. Unfortunately, because things are done so systematically the result is that we were deployed to somewhere that didn't actually need us.
In Fact, we were going to be more of a nuisance whilst also putting ourselves at risk. Luckily discussing with a co-worker and bosses we were able to use our common sense and conserve ourselves for when we are actually useful. Phew!

I did however have a minor panic about getting the chuck from my work for standing up for myself and other staff but the absence from work has maybe given me some balls, either that or because it was all over the phone. People are braver behind screens. Much braver and completely unaware of what their actions may cause.

Therapy

Today was another good day, same as yesterday. Lots of sunshine (yesterday especially) including building a tent to play in, painting the fence (again) and no self-destructive behaviour towards my hair.

In fact, I ordered new shampoo which arrived today. It's the same shampoo one of my work friends uses and as I washed my hair with it today, I got ridiculous memories of daft conversations that we had after swimming lessons with me slyly borrowing shampoo from her as I would always forget mine.

Literally every week. Maybe I wasn't actually doing it by accident. My hair may have subliminally made me not take mine so it could be looked after properly one day of the week, all at the expense of my lovely friend. She wasn't the only one, in fact every time I entered the pool for work, I would genuinely forget so whoever was unlucky enough to be in the showers would be at peril from the shampoo thief aka me.

I would love to say I did it on purpose, but I didn't. In Fact, a few weeks before the lockdown after showering I couldn't find my clothes. I got half dressed as I had some shorts, but I had no other clothing and I had to return to work immediately after.

Luckily my workplace is so damn lovely that as I'm running around with a towel and some odd shorts my workmates and boss are laughing at my ridiculousness. The customers giving me strange looks didn't find it so funny I imagine, or maybe they did and felt rude laughing directly to my face. Either way I am a bit forgetful in life as it seems. Without my google calendar I'm pretty sure I wouldn't be at work or nursery at the times I am supposed to be.

Last night I was lucky enough to be on a video chat with 2 of my favourite work friends "working". We had been assigned some work to do from home which was a great excuse to catch up about the world we were living in. It was then that I realised how much I appreciate my job again. Not for the fact that I can pay bills and buy birthday presents and all that jazz but for the brilliant people I work with.

I have at least 3 shifts a week that make my job fun, especially therapy Thursday, a day in which we moan about every bug bear in our lives getting it out of our systems to be happy. We all have our flaws which we moan about plenty but in essence it's mostly all fun and a pretty decent gig with minimal stress. For my work friends I am extremely grateful.

For now, this will have to be my therapy Thursday.

Today we did so much that made us happy. Our morning walk in the woods collecting sticks and listening to the birds chirping, until my youngest fell out of a tree.

Bit of an exaggeration, he slipped between a couple of big branches and scraped his leg. This however did end with me carrying him the whole way home as he moaned about his sore leg and his brother riding his scooter.

Oh, to be in the mind of a child where the worries are as minimal as this. I got a decent wake up call to this today after this trip to the woods and after multiple falling outs from the two boys. However, it was mostly prominent when we played a couple of new board games. The excitement of getting a new game to play, I imagine would equate to getting a new car in adult life.

The sheer eagerness of trying your hardest to win the game and outsmart your dad would equate to passing a university degree. The distraught tantrum that ensued after dad mixed up the cards in a memory game, making it so much harder would equate to getting a virus on your work computer.

Their problems seem minimal to us now but as a child I remember feeling emotions so much more deeply. The little things were big because we didn't really know what big was at that point, but every emotion we feel once again in adult life without even recognising it because the issue we have is "so much more" than what we felt then. But I'm not really sure it is. We just have a bigger role in creating these problems rather than them being thrust upon us.

I feel like I live with three kids most of the time and I'm sure most people feel this way, or I sure hope so anyway.

We were in the back garden building a campfire to roast marshmallows. I quickly had to tell my eldest off for kicking a ball near the fire, our garden isn't that big at the back, so I had terrible visions of accidentally setting the whole street on fire. Anyway, he obliged and helped get the right sized sticks.

5 minutes later my partner joins us in the garden and immediately starts kicking a ball like he's Ronaldo. I don't even get a chance to speak and my eldest tells him off, to which I am rather proud, and he apologies.
An apology doesn't mean an end to the behaviour though apparently. The fire grows and we begin with our marshmallows and low and behold, he's still kicking a fucking ball. This time I tell him and remind him of the example he is setting for the kids and "you wonder why they don't listen" conversation begins.

Twenty minutes later and we let the fire die down but strangely enough he's still kicking a ball around the garden. Do as I say, not as I do, run through my mind and I hold back everything I have inside from shouting "you are a fanny" across the garden. Mostly because I know my youngest will repeat these words and only these words for the rest of the week but also because is it that big of a deal? no. The inner voice in me then repeats "well if it's not that much of a big deal why can't he just bloody stop?!"
Not only do I battle with the world, my partner and my kids but also now battle with myself. I am also a fanny.

Reprieve

This week seems to have flown past. Nothing is really changing apart from the death toll and the fear of impending doom. We currently sit at just shy of 9000 people dead in the UK.

What I have been questioning is where the line is drawn between guilt and civil duty. When can we say no and when is it our obligation to join without doubt? This has obviously happened many times before in history, however there was less choice. In the war the guilt to become a soldier lay more with men in particular. Their duty was to fight for their country and to leave everything they had without an idea of ever returning.

Those days were different in a million ways. Equal opportunities and house husbands of this generation has made life more stable across the board. Well not completely but in some respects.

The selfish and scared person in me craves the old way of living at times, where the male goes to work and the woman stays at home, however I also love a challenge so I'd probably have to be home-schooling my kids and learning 5 new languages and doing a degree to feel like I was achieving my potential. (I know, rather big headed of myself. Aim high and all that)

Anyway, I have been questioning these things in life as the opportunity to work in the care home has resurrected itself. I received a phone call from the very kind care manager trying to resolve our previous issues as he did with the other members of staff.

So, although I had very strong ideas about protecting my family, they were pushed to the side to go where help is needed.

Well so far all I have agreed to is an induction, but I know that is not all it will be. Guilt is the cause, and the guilt trip doesn't come from the low level sources. My boss and the service manager have guilt from above, to push to do their jobs.

The hierarchy of the system is a bit skewed. It wouldn't take much to break a link in the chain though so if one person at a higher level says no, and wants to protect those under them, it would put a breaker in the system. I suppose however they wouldn't be classed as good leaders and certainly not money makers.

I have given myself some grace at least as I will not work between two services at once (try and limit cross contamination) as I have no idea how I have been so lucky to have two reassignments and some work to do from home, however I will take this as a compliment.

It's amazing what you can convince yourself you are doing for greater good.

Anyway, onto something a little more interesting. As all doctors surgeries etc. are for essentials only we received a call from my youngest paediatrician from the nearest hospital. We were supposed to be at an appointment, but they are all conducted through phone calls now.
It turned out not bad and it actually saved a lot of time and hassle because although I said nearest hospital, it's still 45 minutes away and that's only if you nip on when you're driving.

So, because we have numerous appointments for following up with my youngest and occasionally my eldest it means a whole day rearranged and a long trip that we usually turn into a day at the cinema or something. It is good fun, and it puts a spin on something that can be pretty nerve wracking into something totally brilliant.

So, I received the call, and we were able to discuss how well he is doing and any immediate concerns, which I did have. I worry about his legs as he is constantly complaining about how sore his legs are and how he can't move. In fact, I'm probably a bit cruel trying to make fun of the situation and I copy his "my can't walk" moan in an attempt to get him to carry on moving.

However, as I tend to think that I am paranoid, even if I don't have a lot of reasons to think I'm wrong (especially with this kid), I under dramatize it for them and try to make them resilient. It may sound harsh if there is generally a problem, but until we know there is then they have to be able to cope with things that are difficult.

Ok so back to the conversation the doc says he's not too worried yet but wouldn't completely say it was just growing pains. The frequency is a lot, and he asks if there are any other symptoms such as a fever, to which I reply "erm not that I can think of just now".

He says ok you can give me a call back in a few weeks if things haven't changed, things have gotten worse or there are any other symptoms such as fatigue, off of food or a fever.

The phone call ends and I'm thinking hmm. There are other symptoms, I just wouldn't have called them symptoms. He's always tired and is a fussy eater anyway, but the tired thing has definitely been prominent. After my phone call I carry on with my day and kind of push it to the side thinking I will probably be phoning him in a few weeks anyway.

A day later and I think "ahh ill just look it up" I know, it's stupid for some, but I wouldn't be able to not try and find a solution or a cause in the most exhaustive manor possible.

So, I look it up, leukaemia is an option, but really, I don't imagine that is even close to the cause. The symptoms don't fit, and it's too farfetched. Also, we don't get given what we can't handle... and that would not be something I could handle, my limit is well before that.

However, a familiar word catches my eye and I see lupus. It's linked to the liver disease we have, and the symptoms are almost exact. I am almost convinced this is what it is, however, I can't immediately jump to this conclusion without the consultation of the doctor, which is fine. At least I have an idea of what's going on. The symptoms feel similar to what I experience and with a little bit more research it could possibly be hereditary. It's an avenue, probably not the right one but I'll take it and see what the next few weeks hold.

After my crazy mum reaction to a simple phone call, I believe I need to carry on as before which I do, however I'm just a tad more aware this is not just in my head. Thank goodness.

Its easter weekend and I have pretty much forgot so as a last ditch attempt at making it a bit fun we repaint our living room windows (easter egg theme) with a thank you message for the postman who has had to deliver loads of packages to us recently because of my eldest's upcoming birthday. They do an amazing job and one in particular makes sure packages are held for us even if they are addressed wrong by my mum. She tried her best, and it was amazing.

I've kind of zoned out of the world for now and am zoned in on the kids, possibly in protection mode. It's worth it and I don't particularly feel the need to apologise to people for not replying as I would expect the same from others. However, I do in part feel bad, but grateful for the peace.

My reception friend would be perfect in this situation as we enjoy just being in each other's company, without the pressure of having to make conversation. I seem to make these types of friends often as the two friends I have who moved away are very similar and are just amazing to be around.

I got a text from one of my oldest friends at about 10pm. She lives nearby and has dropped some easter eggs for the kids and us off at the doorstep. Turns out she did it quite a while earlier in the day and forgot to say, probably expecting us to be outside at some point.
 We weren't, so at 10pm I ran down to the door and hoped it hadn't been raining and found a bag full of chocolate easter gifts which I brought inside and replied to her with a very grateful message. She thinks of everything in advance, including my kids. In Fact, she goes shopping for their presents in October for Christmas. I wish I had the forward planning that she does as I might be somewhere like Nicola Sturgeon right now. Well probably not but it's nice to dream.

Crap, I've just remembered I haven't replied to my gran after messaging her this morning and feel guilty as anything (can't say hell because I would then feel guilty about that too.)
I've lost the opportunity to have a conversation with her and it's so frustrating. I miss them so badly. We managed to zoom in the other day with the whole family including my grandparents. It was chaotic and mad but was just so good to see their faces and feel like I was in their company. I think that is what I miss the most. Oh crap, I forgot to phone my dad back too.

Instead of doing all these important things I sat down to write. Probably for the best so that when I do talk to people it's not some crazy ass long conversation about my worries.
Anyway, I'm out for the night (not out out), I'm done, so I can go and catch up on all the crap I ignored today.

Busy mind and a lonely heart

Time is passing so quickly once again. The last time I even had a chance to sit down and write was about 1 week ago. I think. Don't quote me on that.

It's been such a busy week between planning for my eldest's fifth birthday, work and the constant turmoil of the glorious pandemic. Life hasn't stopped or slowed down, but it's certainly more manageable. For me personally mental health is more manageable because we are in a stable situation. I know it's not the same for everyone and this is a chaotic mess, however I've reached a point where I'm enjoying life again.

The obvious issues in my life stick out like a sore thumb, but the happiness is also like a shining star and by far outweighs the rest of the plumb.

Having something to look forward to certainly makes life a lot more exciting and meaningful. It has gotten to the point of squeezing things into a day and forgetting to do a million other things. However, it's lovely things I get to squeeze in and the stuff I keep forgetting is the online work to do for my job. Luckily none of it is particularly time dependent.

This week alone we have went on a million bike rides, watched about 15 movies, repainted our windows twice, been shopping, had shopping delivered, organised a mini birthday party (with no outside participants), painted ourselves and a million pictures, made a doctor's outfit, did an easter egg hunt in the rain, painted eggs (that are still sitting in the fridge), played in the paddling pool, ate cake for breakfast, made muffins, playdough and played Lego a million times. Strangely enough, we still haven't finished painting our fence. (How long ago did this begin? I have no idea anymore)

I miss my grandparents even more than ever. I miss my nephews and my sisters and brother.
I really even just want a day with them having a big party or something.

Thief

Some things never change. No matter the circumstances of the world, people and their priorities don't change and it's hard to see certain parts of behaviour as anything other than ugly.

I don't see people as generally ugly or bad people, however as time goes on people can reveal un-endearing behaviour that I tend to perceive as ugly.

This type of behaviour can totally change my perception of people, not to the point of not talking to people but trust doesn't stretch very far, and I find it hard to participate in particular conversations. So even though the world is in a pandemic, people don't always change. The same problems all the damn time.

Some do and the generosity I have seen for the past few weeks has been amazing. People willing to look after the vulnerable, giving meals and shopping and work for free. The counter-effect of the current government is people being forced to look out for each other. The government won't provide, therefore, the communities will and after all of this is over, it should continue this way, but instead of having no help, all of the supplementations could be aimed at communities. Almost like a reward scheme. The more you do for your community that is relevant the more opportunities you create for everyone the more support you get.

This may not make sense really and probably wouldn't work in our world, however something to that effect would go down a treat.

This is also where the guilt for not wanting to work in the care home comes from. Where in essence is my solid reason for not doing my part to help. Really, I have no good excuse not to be out there working with whoever. I know if I was to contract it and die, my kids would survive and be looked after.

However, if I was to go out there and pass it on to someone else and they died, I don't know if I could live with that guilt. For now, anyway I am being a coward and not contacting my work, keeping a low profile and doing the things I was assigned. Not a long term solution, but it will work for now.

In amongst the days off, one of the things we did was build a set of football goals out of scraps of wood and an old tent inner. It was brilliant fun, and the boys were delighted as they could see it coming together, but in true "just my luck" style I managed to injure myself. I was feeling on top of the world, having almost completed this project and as I am smashing the last nail in, I miss aim and wallop my finger! I cursed myself then my eldest, having watched what I had done, started saying "calm down mummy, it's ok".

Reluctantly I realise he's right, I need to chill the feck out, but it's so damn hard! Eventually I chill out, get the kids to bed, and head down stairs to inspect the damage. My finger is pulsing, and I can't have it point towards the ground because the pain is unreal.

It feels ready to explode so I decide I need to release the pressure. I can already feel my face starting to drain and I began to feel like the man in Edvard munch "the scream" painting.

I got the needle and it seemed to be really hard to push through and then pop. A big spot of blood popped out, but not enough to relieve the pressure. However, a rather more pressing issue emerged as I started to wobble, hands shaking and head spinning. I go to the living room and put my legs up on the sofa and lie on the floor, only after I've texted my friend explaining the ridiculous predicament.

After a minute or so she replies telling me to text if I need her to come over and watch me from the window. It was a lovely gesture, and I laughed a lot before I finally felt ok again.

This was the same friend who had knocked herself out in the middle of the night, so she understood the situation rather quickly. May I add, I was the only adult in the house, a fine example of the prime opportunity for this crap not to happen.

Anyway, I'm learning to live with my stupid mistakes and my kids are heroes at adopting to live in the pandemic. They literally don't give much of a crap. My eldest has a decent understanding of it and if anyone comes too close, he tells them to step back because he doesn't want to make them sick or them to make us sick. It's cute and because he's little people are taken aback and tend to listen a bit more than they would if I was to scream it in their faces.

I think at this rate we could live this way for quite a while, and possibly buy a house across the road for my grandparents so we could see them at least!

Our large bike runs make life rather interesting. We biked to the beach and stopped to do some rock climbing which the kids adored and became the most excited I've ever seen them. It was lovely and enchanting to feel like I was actually beginning to understand my kids for who they are.

A friend also dropped a few things off at our house the other day, one being a bike helmet and the other a pair of flippers. I know this would maybe be classed as junk, but not in this house. The kids have worn the flippers everywhere possible and have almost only taken the bike helmets off to go to sleep. Such little things amuse them so well.

My eldest also dreams of being a diver when he is older, so we had a whole morning of him naked, with flippers, goggles and a helmet on jumping off my sofa.

The pandemic is taking a lot and giving things we didn't even realise we needed. It has given me in particular the time with my kids (which I asked for and caused the pandemic...or so I thought) as well as the boundaries to enjoy them without the interruption of others. It means we can't go to soft play and call it quality time, or we can't take them to the cinema and say it's a treat because due to the time we have now, nothing else would compare.

It has taken a lot, mostly time with my family and friends. I'm one of the lucky ones who still has an income, but for many it has taken their livelihood. All the zero hour contracts across the country have nothing to fall back on. I do believe most of the contracts are in the care sector (could be wrong) therefore they will have more work than you could imagine for now. That is until they are classed as unskilled once again.

It has taken one of my favourite love stories (my friend and their boyfriend). I found out the other night that the pair had separated, and I was gutted, although I heard the reasons why and totally understood, but still. I wanted something to last.

It has also taken so much money. I keep thinking of my work who have no income as of now as we are completely shut down, in fact their outgoings haven't changed much but we have no income. I'm grateful I'm not the boss at this moment in time.

It has also taken my money. Although I haven't been shopping as often as I usually would, I have spent a fortune on food. My usual trip to Tesco would be £60 and since the pandemic it hasn't been less than £97. There are no deals on, and certain items are harder to get, so an extra pound on something you would usually spend 50p on really adds up.

The biggest thing it has taken obviously has been lives. 16060 lives to be exact in the UK, but worldwide 164,391 so far and those numbers aren't exactly accurate. To put that into perspective it doesn't touch the death toll on wars and things such as the plague, however it's far more people than we could imagine to lose to something so invisible and so hard to diagnose apparently.

Hopefully we never again in our lifetime see something so dramatic that has brought the world to its knees in terms of finances and lifestyle. Where we are currently in Scotland seems to be well enough managed for a lockdown that we are coping. Mainly because it's so sparsely populated, and we live in the country compared to people who live on top of each other in the cities. This, I am grateful for.

I am also grateful for having a birthday with my son where we only had to please him. It sounds ridiculous but we didn't have to plan a party and take time away from him to do this. He helped bake his own cake and we wrapped his presents and decorated the house when he was in bed. We enjoyed our time with him celebrating directly with his wants and desires which were already limited to pretty much what he could see. I did feel for our family who wanted to celebrate with him and couldn't, however he understood and knew that after this is all over, we can make up with a million hugs and snogs as he puts it.

For now, life isn't too bad for us personally. I imagine this would change if someone we knew didn't cope with the virus well. Once again, for now I'm going to live in our bubble.

On a brighter note, today I ran a 5k (as I was nominated to) and did it in a similar time as the one I ran when I was 18. 8 years later and I must be of similar fitness. Although I do think I was breathing out my arse a lot more this time.

Lava bridge

So, I pulled my finger out my butt yesterday after having a complete downer day. I couldn't gather the energy or desire to even think of something to do. I had fun ideas and I didn't even want to binge watch tv. I just felt bleurgh, which is different to meh apparently as I found out. Thankfully that day passed eventually, and we were a bit more productive.

I finally phoned the care home and organised my induction for Wednesday, and I contacted Kieran's doctor about his knees. I've put this off forever and after the phone consultation a few weeks ago I thought, ok enough is enough. We also finally decorated some pictures for my partner as it's his birthday soon, unfortunately I wasn't quick enough to think of his presents so he will get his hoover and Fitbit in about a week. Who doesn't love a late birthday present?
I ordered him a chain as well, but it will be more of a Christmas present at the rate it is being delivered at.
I'm not complaining, I can't really complain about anything really.

I am on a complete high just now from having such a happy day. We saw numerous people that we haven't in a while, and we did things we would probably normally do. Nothing really went to plan or panned out the way we would expect, and it was brilliant.

So, for starters I had been up until about 1am thinking about doing my induction at the care home, this then led to me sleeping like a brick until 7am. Unfortunately for me my kids were up not long after 6 and had gotten fed up with trying to wake me so decided to go make themselves breakfast.
I woke at 7am to the sound of plates banging together. I crept downstairs and heard the whispers of them working together, no fights or arguments and two bowls of cereal on the table. Along with this were 2 demolished yoghurts and 1 plate of toast with what looked like 1kg of butter on it and a dollop of jam (the second lot of toast was cooking in the toaster).
My eldest was dressed in his police outfit and my youngest was on the worktop "tidying" the dishes. I was rather pleasantly surprised as they had

looked after each other well, they were eating healthy food and had not chosen to have chocolate for breakfast! Their futures are bright.

After this we picked my partner up from work and we got ready for our day. I nipped to the care home for my induction and returned to some happy, chilled out kids asking if I wanted to go to the "bridge of lava". I agreed and made a packed lunch not realising the journey was about 8 and ½ km.

Anyway, the bike run went so well, and we arrived at the lava bridge where we ate our picnic and played by the river. It was beautiful and felt kind of like a mirage. The landscape just made you feel like you were a million miles away and was so peaceful. The kids were delighted and explored until it was time to carry on and get home.

All was going well until we came down a gritty hill and I skidded a little but held my bike upright.

This was fine but of course my eldest did the same and came flying off his bike. Lots of tears and crying but not a scratch on him, woohoo I thought as we carried on. My partner 2 minutes later asked me to check his bike because it "felt funny". I had a quick look and saw a completely flat back tyre. Damn and we still had another 4km to get home.

We managed to get home about an hour and a half later through pushing and still trying to pedal the much heavier bike. The relief of even being in our own street was immense and after a cup of tea the world was ok again.

I ballsed up our dinner, well not for us all, but for the kids. Making tacos on a Wednesday is evidently not ok. In Fact, making tacos any day is not ok (according to the kids).

We muddled through dinner and had an ice bucket challenge to do. My partner and myself were both nominated so we set it all up and played a prank on my unbeknown partner.

Life lesson here too: don't let your kids in on secrets because they can't keep them. After about a million hints from my eldest that it was only water in his bucket, he was still none the wiser that we had put slime in his bucket. We poured our tubs at the same time, and he was genuinely gutted that we had outsmarted him. The destruction on his face was brilliant. Is it bad that I took so much joy in his dismay, I sure hope not because it was magic.

After this brilliant day I showed the kids some pictures I had taken of the day and I always used to think that it was stupid to relive the memories almost immediately after they were created, but today I was wrong. At this point I was tired and a bit grumpy, but the pictures literally lifted me sky high.

The utter awe I was in earlier at the bridge came back like the sun glowing. It lifted my mood and raised my patience level. I wonder if this could be a continuous thing that would happen each time, I look at the pictures.

I hope so as it reminded me of those silly moments after my kids were born. I would be sitting with them sleeping in my arms scrolling through pictures of them with sheer delight or tucking my kids into bed and then going into my own room to stare at pictures of them. We maybe don't all do this, and I rarely do it now unless I've completed most of my tasks for the day. It's sad I know, but I can't help myself.

On a not so great note my papa is not well. In Fact, they felt he was so unwell they took him to hospital last night. This would not usually be a massive deal but when there's a pandemic and the hospital is 1 hour away, it's a bit unnerving.

I sure hope he's ok for a million reasons but especially now because he and my gran were spending their lockdown kitting out a caravan for their 5 grandchildren to play in when this is all over. Their house is like a sanctuary as it is so isolated and calming. In fact, I'm not even sure it's the house, probably just their company that is so relaxing.

So much of the world is unknown right now and our death toll has risen to 18,100 approximately so far. The good deeds are still expanding and people looking out for each other is growing a natural kindness. One thing that is highlighted often is the animals who live in captivity and basically a lockdown for their whole lives. They don't even have the choice to break the rules, even if they wanted to. We complain about the possibility of a few months in this crisis when we don't know the half of what we have already inflicted on the animals we supposedly care for.

The world really needs to change and the possibility of a year in lockdown might give us just enough time to regain balance in a lot of systems.

Fuzzy head

This week has been a strange and frustrating one. Have you ever felt like there is a big fuzzy tangled mess inside your head and to get to it you have to travel through the thickest fog and smoke? Maybe not everyone has felt like this, but this week I have.

It has been so confusing because lots of interesting things have happened and we have had a lot of laughs, but all I have wanted to do is have a little cry and I can't. Not because I can't cry in front of my kids, because I know I can definitely do that, but I just physically can't connect my brain to my body no matter how much I want to.

My youngest had an appointment to get bloods done at the hospital on Friday, all to do with his knees and I was evidently more anxious than he was. I had to pick my partner up from work on the way there so he could stay with my eldest and drop him off on the way back. Usually, we would make a day of it, but nothing is open and it's impossible. My partner still managed to go Pokémon hunting with my eldest, so it was all good.

The staff at the hospital were brilliant and minimal. A couple of nurses took his bloods and after trying his arm for quite a while she asked if she could use his foot. Even she cringed when she said it and although I physically said yes, my body felt like it was turning itself inside out at the thought.

He's had a cannula in his foot before and I know how uncomfortable it was for him so my only thought was that it wasn't staying in, quick in and out and the pain would be over.
In the end he was as brilliant as he could be. He cried and got upset because they had to wiggle the needle a lot to get any form of blood out. In Fact, the pain was enough to make him scream and pee everywhere. My heart wanted to leap out my chest and hold him so tightly, but we must soldier on.

This ordeal obviously has stuck with me and reminded me of all the pain he has been through in the past and stunned me into a place of coping. This place has no emotions and has no voice, just silence. It's a lonely place and I'm glad I don't live there permanently.

It's bad to want some result other than nothing. I want the blood results to give us an answer to why he finds life so hard, and I want it to be something manageable rather than a "we don't know, nothing we can do" because so many times in life, not knowing is so much more stressful than problem solving.

I also started my redeployment to the care home today and enjoyed the easy going attitude of the place. The staff were lovely, and it wasn't as scary as I thought. As far as new jobs go, it's a low stress one so far. Things may change in the future but I'm hanging on to the idea that I've struck lucky really.

I'm also a bit behind on the work I was sent home from my boss. She also sent a document to look over and I couldn't gain access to it, so rather than being proactive I did nothing. I've still done nothing, and I feel like a tit for it, but this has felt like a rough week.

Time waits for no man. Time is the thing I wished for before the pandemic and even now that the world has slowed down, I have gotten myself into the rut of having no time again, which in essence tells you that I have always had the time. I just don't manage it correctly.

I haven't written much recently because this was my saviour previously and now, I don't have the energy to even bring myself to think. luckily for now my laptop has a spell check!
Also, the death toll has now reached 20,000 and apparently, it's taking a dip in deaths. The government is calling this a victory and the rest of this country knows its buffering time, a lag or glitch time waiting for the weekend numbers to actually be put into the system. Apparently, there is a choice to never work weekends, who would have known!

Just say no

So, we are 6 and a half weeks into lockdown, and it has become a new normal. It's peaceful and quite pleasant. The only unlucky reminder of the previous world is the occasional update from work and a few days working in the care home I was re-designated to. I haven't been able to write at all. No matter how hard I tried I have been exhausted with worry and stupid fear. After my first shift at the care home, I became angry at my employer for putting me in that position. That was before I realised that it was actually me who put me in that position, no one else.

No is such a simple word to say, in the correct situation. Some people find saying no extremely easy, almost like a reflex in fact. I am not one of these people. When I say no what usually follows is a ton of guilt until I cave or feel bad for a while. Depending on how high it is on my list of priorities depends on how quick I cave or not.
It's crap but has also led me to meet some amazing and interesting people. On the flipside it's also led to some strange situations and people but some doors you open can lead you to great places and behind others there is a weirdo. Most doors are weirdos.

I got a call today which took a decision out of my hands and removed me from my redeployment. It was relieving. I wanted to contact them prior to this and say I didn't want to come back, however the amazing staff and awaiting clients prevented me from doing this. Whilst I was on shift on Friday a resident who was supposed to still be in isolation due to a positive covid-19 test came to me in the laundry room. I was wearing minimal PPE (gloves and a plastic apron) and had a short conversation with her. She was returning property to the correct place and would have been a totally harmless act as she was lonely and in need of other company.
I initially didn't think too much of it as I had been having a lovely day with the staff on shift, however I soon realised when she was talking that she may still be contagious.

Such an innocent and sweet act prompted many issues as I was now put at risk when not particularly necessary. I brought it up at the team check-in meeting and the staff were a little shocked. Not majorly as they work in this environment all of the time but enough to prompt a response. I went to sort out my shifts for the following week to find that they were not particularly short staffed at all, and I would be extra therefore I left the decision for a few days.

Luckily for me I didn't need to contact the care home as my work friend called first. It couldn't come sooner as I have a pounding headache and feel exhausted and have done so since the day after my last shift. Great. Probably dehydration, but who knows.

Either way we are unlucky enough to live in a country that under-reacts to everything. Admittable, I try my best to do this as well so that if it does become worst case scenario then I can officially start freaking the fuck out.

I do this with all aspects as much as possible, however I also feel deep down that the panicking psychopath lives just under my skin hidden from sight.

The paediatrician called on Friday too and said that my youngest's blood results were back and all was ok apart from one, therefore we would need to retest him to make sure it wasn't from squeezing the blood out of him. Once again, the doctors tend not to give you the full story so that we don't turn to DR google, which is of course what I would do, but the lack of information is infuriating.

Nonetheless I can't change it, it happens so often you learn to read between the lines, which is probably worse. It's like reading a dictionary with half of the information blacked out.

For example, during our stay in the hospital with meningitis, it wasn't until my youngest had been put in the high dependency unit for 3 days did, I find out what the cause was.

This information was gathered from a general conversation from a nurse who was telling me to get some sleep. 3 weeks later at home we found out from our health visitor that he had sepsis too. Some pretty decent information was left out, however in that case I was only grateful that the amazing health professionals were making my son well.

During that stay there were a few nurses who made the situation bearable. There were 2 people who I never wanted to see in my life again, one a doctor and one a student nurse, but resenting a student nurse is not particularly fair obviously because they are still learning and most likely don't have children of their own to know how you are feeling.

The doctor however I don't excuse completely. I do minimally as everyone can make mistakes however this one made a few. I asked him if there would be any repercussions from the meningitis health wise or physically. He said no, everything should be fine.

3 weeks later and we were back as his liver hadn't been performing well (which he forgot to mention) when we left and had gotten worse. To add to this when we came back, he was asked to put in a cannula in the middle of the night as my sons had come out. This was a great hassle for him but rather than getting it over with quickly as soon as my son started to cry, he sent the supporting nurse to another far away department to get some sucrose (sugary water) to soothe him. Low and behold after 10 minutes of screaming the sugary water didn't help and he had to carry on regardless. By this point I was angry and so was the nurse he sent on a wild goose chase.

Like I said we all make mistakes, I just hope we don't encounter him again, unless he has learned a lot from these situations. How sad is that, I still hold a grudge after 2 years. However, it's hard to forget someone who hurts your kid. Having a child literally makes someone else become the centre of your soul. The more you have, the more you give away. I refuse to have any more as I don't think my nerves could take it. Plus, the two I have feel pretty perfect to me.

We have done so much this week as always or it feels like a lot anyway. All the games and entertainment provided by mum and dad inc. I do love family time and the bonds that have been built even further with my kids and even my partner. The things I used to get annoyed at have slipped to the back of my mind and I seem to notice his kind gestures a lot more than before. He has always been good with the kids and housework, but it's so much more obvious now without the chaos of normal life.

I find it hard to keep up with the outside world and don't actually remember the last time I had a proper conversation with someone not in my household. It sounds and feels bad, but the brain fog has turned into a brick wall that I can't break through. It's like when you leave a job to start a new one, keeping in touch with previous workmates becomes impossible because you don't see them every day. I still miss my people but can't communicate effectively through technology. I'm a bit of a shit friend, which I always knew as I don't connect the thought of missing someone with actual action. Texting someone "thinking of you" sounds a bit weird, especially if you were to send it 7 times a day. To those who fly through my mind on a daily basis, I miss you and I wish I were a better friend. I hope you are all well and coping with life as it is. Reported death toll: 28734. Likely much higher as evidently all news is fake news.

I wish a better day for everyone tomorrow and I'm going to take my brick head for a long sleep.
 Stay safe.

Everything happens
for a reason

So much can happen in a short space of time. How ridiculous is that statement, of course it can.
Anyway, this week a lot has happened in the scale of my life, it wouldn't be classed as much on the grand scale of the universe, but for me it's plenty.

After being taken out of my redeployment I was told to be on standby ready to go back at any point as if it was some superhero mission. I agreed to wait by my bat signal even though I had been planning to call and say that I wasn't going to go back.

I then got a phone call from the GP who decided that neither myself nor my kids would be on the shielding list for covid as we didn't actually have the liver disease that is on our record.
Someone else at the GP surgery then contacted us and overturned the decision, so I received a text and a phone call to let me know there was a letter in the post.

The letter is 6 weeks late, however at least I am not actually as crazy and paranoid as I thought. Well, that is still debatable.

It's pointless almost but I suppose now that the virus seems to have properly hit our area of the country it may not be too late. I do wish my gut feeling was enough to convince myself and others that I shouldn't be working in risky places, but rules are rules and unless someone actually stands up and decides the rules then we are all kind of wandering about with no idea of who's really in charge and by the time that someone decides, it's already too late. We pass the buck, because it's easier to blame someone else rather than put our own heads on the block.

Anyone who puts themselves up there eventually gets taken down and smeared as if everything that has gone wrong is on them. However, according to my friends everything is covid-19 fault and I can't disagree.

I also had my youngest to get more blood done this week and he was a trooper. All week I could feel myself being nervous but as it came to getting them done, the lovely nurses did a finger prick test instead and we put on Pokémon go and he just sat there quite happy.

The nurses did acknowledge that evidently there is something going on for the doctor to deem it necessary to have bloods done during a pandemic and that felt like a win in the argument to prove I'm not nuts. I don't actually feel like I have to prove this, luckily for me growing up I had parents who encouraged me to stand out and not be afraid to be different.

It did lead to a lot of bullying for about 6 years, but luckily for me (again) I had a big sister who would stick up for me and nail those mfs* so that I didn't have to.

Everything happens for a reason. The reason may be totally screwed up and twisted but it all does. I'm not sure if I would say this if a death was involved but events in life tend to link, or so I find anyway. For example, I got an interview for my dream job when I was 20. It was an apprenticeship with an oil company designing equipment and rigs. I know it sounds rather boring, but I just wanted to be a designer of anything and to me this was a dream.

I went to the whole day's interview and proceeded with the millions of tests that they put in front of us trying my best and then came the face-to-face part. I was doing very well (judging by the questions and looks on their faces) as I mostly spoke about my month trip to Ghana where we literally did so much stuff and learned so much.

I spoke about the adjustments back to life here in Scotland and how I had actually loathed coming back to this type of society. They were impressed and then actually said "wow, which was so interesting, I suppose we better ask you some of these questions from the sheet" and I thought Yass! I've nailed it.

Obviously, I spoke too soon because honest me kicked in and I rambled about how working alone was great and working in a team was good too as long as it was a good team who could work together and not be pricks.

I said something to that effect, and it dawned on me quickly what I was saying, but I couldn't take it back and I couldn't stop. As I left, I could feel the failure on everyone's faces in the room, especially mine. I was hopeful as usual and thought, maybe they will overlook all that crap and see what an asset I could be.

Meh. definitely not.

I did not get that job and I didn't even call back to find out why because I knew. However, what this did lead me to was coming back home and continuing looking for something new. Less than a month later I fell pregnant with my eldest. Thankfully I didn't have an underpaid apprenticeship at the time, and I received maternity leave and had a job to go back to after.

I had also begun on a much more exciting journey in my life than I could ever have imagined.

Not going to lie, I had always seen myself as someone with a big successful career and all these cool fast cars and beautiful houses. Now I can't even imagine the loneliness that that would have brought and how boring life would have been. Although I would never have been pooped on numerous times or be half as sleep deprived as I am now, I would never wish for that life ever, especially not over what I have now. Everything happens for a reason.

Always bugs

I don't know if I've written this yet, but I am very grateful for my kids apart from when they are boys. Long story short: my eldest placed a snail on my leg the other day. I was sitting in the sun enjoying life with a cup of tea and he came up and said "mum look hahaha" and put the snail on my leg. I screamed and threw the snail back at him, to which he didn't notice because he was laughing so hard.

The kid is five and he already knows how to entertain himself and piss off his mum. I laughed a lot afterwards and thought to myself "you are creating a bad habit" as soon as he realises that this kind of crap is funny, then that's all I am ever going to get. We are in need of something more female in our home, because I am the only one and even then, I'm not that great at it. However, there is also no more room for anyone or anything in this house and I'm not doing the baby thing again. I feel I have done my bit in populating the world with beautiful people, it's not my turn anymore.

Last ridiculous thing we did today. We set up a line for a snail nightclub. We came back from a walk in the rain and saw that there were millions of snails in the garden. My youngest was a tad scared so sat just inside the front door with me (being the bouncers) and my eldest gathered them all up and lined them up on the step.
We had a couple of guys we couldn't let in because they were scrapping, one who was giving us cheek so was refused entry and some who wouldn't show us their face, so they were turned away too. A hilarious ten minutes of my life that I think my kids were oblivious to.

All's well that ends well for now in our bubble.
On the bigger bubble: death toll: 31,587

Not ending so well at all, and now people are protesting, having to stay home. Fuckwits everywhere. Meanwhile in Scotland the daily banter grows with roses are red poems. If you've not seen it yet, google it, it's brilliant.

You're crazy

This morning started off well. After receiving my son's shielding orders my partner came home from work and we made him strip at the front door. Unfortunately, it was 8am so not many people were around to witness the full Monty.

He seemed annoyed and fed up, however, who knows what is actually going on because in this house I think he must think sharing feelings is illegal. We let him get on with cleaning the house and carry on with having no plans for the day. The kids later cheer him up by jumping on his back from the sofa and throwing fake poop at him. Cheers me up too apparently.

We get showered and dressed to look good for all the people we won't see today and as we head downstairs I somehow take a flying leap on the last section and throw cold tea on every surface (especially the white walls) and cut my ugly finger (the one I whacked with a hammer and lost the nail of). What a great start to the day and then we look outside and it's snowing, in May. 5 minutes previously it was beautiful and sunny. Everything is so unpredictable just now.

I took a trip to Tesco the other day and as per usual (for now) it felt like an expedition into the depths of the Sahara. Just as many scary creatures and feels just as foreign.
It was rather pleasant until I reached the second aisle, and someone kept coming very close behind me. I shuffled on as fast as I could trying not to miss anything because of the dreaded one way system, however I could not shake this person.

I reached the third aisle and decided I would turn around and give them a dirty look. (Checks me super brave) I looked up and just about melted with relief. It was one of my work friends I hadn't seen since lockdown began. She laughed at me and said "I didn't recognise you with your disguise". In my head I'm shouting "you shit!" over and over again and in my heart the overwhelming relief makes me want to cry. We talk a little as we continue around the shop, and I let her pass me. The rest of my shopping trip is a breeze.

In an attempt to make something in my life a little more tolerable I decided to paint a part of our kitchen. This part should be known as the magnet wall. It's a magnet for dirt, food and anything of any colour you could imagine, so I decided in my wisdom to paint it. I knew I didn't have enough paint to cover the whole wall, therefore I only painted a large triangle in grey.

This involved using the blue I used to paint my bathroom and some black chalkboard paint. Sounds simple and in essence it was however as I opened the paint the smell of rotten eggs filled my soul. I'd love to say just my nose, but even thinking about it now it comes back to me and makes me gag.

Anyway, because I had decided to paint, I must carry on. Who knew paint had a use by date? An hour or so later and the paint was dry. A full day later of having the window wide to the sky and 2 candles going with perfume on the heaters and the smell still lingers. I don't care, I'm over it and I just avoid the kitchen more than normal.

What do you do when people around you act like complete tits? Like not just being an idiot on a daily basis doing no harm but making life changing decisions that make you go "wtf?" turning your head upside down trying to make sense of situations.

I know naturally you just leave people to it, however what do you do when this not only encroaches in your own life, but you feel yourself being dragged through and into these events of madness.

Saying no doesn't seem to be enough. Laying out clear boundaries doesn't stick because as soon as the old situation is over and a new crazy one rears its head then apparently the previous rules no longer apply.
This probably sounds like complete and utter drivel however even if I were to explain the ridiculously mad and boring scenario, it would change the following day anyway.

I used to tackle these things in my life by being tolerant and letting people drag me through anything they liked, not having an opinion or sitting on the fence as my sisters would say (which of course frustrated them greatly and probably why I did it for so long was just to annoy the fuck out of them).

My stance changed however when I had my kids. I could no longer willingly be thrust into a situation that I wasn't comfortable with because it was no longer just me. I had two more innocent and vulnerable little men who were impressionable. Everything I did or participated in in life needed to be of value or purpose to growing them into amazing humans without damaging them.

This started off being about one crazy situation in my life and now writing it and reading it back it applies to so much. For years being a doormat or possibly a piece of blue playdough (blue is the best) for anyone who was willing, or who felt that they were pointing me in the right direction.

Multiple situations people believe they know you better than you know yourself and encourage you to do things you may not particularly love. First cigarette, first kiss, first skive in school or something daft to that effect.

For me I think I must have been about 10 or something and a friend (who also bullied me and kicked the shit out of me through school) invited me to play barbies at her house. I went and had fun, but when I wanted to leave, she wouldn't let me. She closed the stair gate and trapped me in her house (I wonder if she's in jail yet for kidnapping).

I know, totally ridiculous and I can't really remember how I got out of there but for some reason the next connected memory in my head is standing in the street with this same girl, her mother shouting from the front door "just punch her" and me with this bewildered look on my face.

Now the next part of this memory I'm not really sure if it's true or not (probably not) but my eldest sister comes in with a flying headbutt to the girl and drags me out the way and we leg it home. Like I said, probably not true, but by all accounts, the way it should have happened.

The good old scheme that we grew up in actually had its own tv show recently because of all the weird and wonderful fannys that live within a 2 km radius.

Anyway, being able to say no is something I never really learned until I had kids, but even then, the limits of who I can say no to are still within minor boundaries (so I'm still a doormat, just to certain people).

My partner is someone I have always been able to say no to, maybe why I've stuck with him for so long. Even when we first met, I felt no bounds in telling him to take a run and jump.

We had only been together about a month or so and we went to a party with friends.
It was all people we both knew very well and felt comfortable around however this party was a bit different as they had all gotten a hold of some drugs and were sniffing who knew what. I was there for about half an hour and said no, I'm out. It was too unpredictable, and I wasn't participating in the new "sporting event" they were all engulfed in, so I thought, `` meh, I'm going home to play Xbox."

I called my step dad at the time and he came to pick me up, however as he arrived he took a nice big look through the window and viewed the day's events.

I got in the car, and he blew his top. My simple argument was "why the fuck do you think I phoned you to come and get me" he calmed down immediately and went home, I thought good, situation dealt with I did the right thing and kept myself safe. Oh, how wrong I was.

The gossip filtered through my family and somehow got to my dad who went into full top fanny mode and decided I needed to come and live with him away from all of the evil. In Fact, it was even muttered that I had gotten into such a bad state that I was now a coke dealer.

Luckily, I also had the balls to say no and didn't even validate the story with any explanation. It was a tough six months with my dad and a situation I have only recently clarified with him at the hospital 10 years later.

(My dad always comes to the hospital when we are in, as I am always on my own with a child. He sits and cheers me up and we apparently put the world to rights. Why I am on my own in the hospital is another argument that we might get to later. Ps. it's a long and boring one.)

Now I've probably delved too much into my life for what is bearable but since this is my kind of therapy, I won't apologise, but I sure hope some ridiculous things like these may have happened to others too, if not something more comical.

I know I'm not the only nut job in this madhouse country.

Walls, balls and falls

So, the past few days life is still very similar, apart from the increasing down mood of this week. I should be happy, I get to stay at home and protect my babies. However, I think I keep staying up far too late and lack of sleep is really kicking my ass.

Today was stressful as something came up that really bugged my happiness. It shouldn't because really, it's not my life. However, watching people ditch every moral they have that they usually preach about daily to satisfy an immediate desire is painful to see.

On the other end of things watching someone doing the exact same thing without ever really having morals about it in the first place is also dire.

(To put into context: wait I can't, I don't know how, maybe just skip past this part.)

It's not the immediate effect of bubbly happiness and joy, it's the future unravelling destruction that you can see happening and can't do a thing about.

This also happened a few weeks ago with one of my nephews. We were out and saw my sister and her family at the local bike track (from a distance) and as they were leaving my nephew went hurtling down a small steep hill into a brick wall.

This wasn't surprising for my nephew who is a mix of billy Connelly and duke kaboom, and who had only just learned to ride his bike that day. Unfortunately, he hadn't learned to use his breaks.

My sister was at the top of the hill completely helpless, his dad at the bottom and slightly too far out of reach and I was on the other end of the embankment shouting for him to use his breaks. He literally crumpled like a tin can, luckily having a helmet to slightly embrace his head. As his parents arrived to scoop him up my sister became horrified after seeing that he had removed his eyebrow from his face.

I could do nothing but stand at a distance and offer nothing. I felt physically sick for 4 hours after the incident, so I have no contemplation of how he felt.

He got checked out and all was ok thanks to his helmet, but he surely rattled all of our nerves.

He's the kid who is going to break every bone in his body and still go back for more. Not going to lie, I'm glad he's not mine. That blessing has been saved for my sister.

After the stresses you go through as a parent or even just being a functioning human it's so important to find the things in life to help you unwind. The things that make your frizzy mess of a brain untangle itself effortlessly. I've struggled to find anything recently that makes me feel ok, however tonight I had a bath.

That sounds ridiculous, I already have 2 baths a day or a shower or something anyway, but this bath was blissful. It wasn't fresh, my kids had already been in it, it was full of toys and was cold by the time I got to it as per usual. The only difference was that I sat in the bath and scrolled on my phone not on social media but playing a game. Nothing exciting but it was my place of sheer comfort and relaxation.

I could feel the yuck of the week peeling off of me the longer I soaked. If you can imagine some perfectly cooked chicken peeling from the bone, that is how I felt, like a cooked chicken. I'm also laughing ridiculously imagining myself as a chicken, cluck cluck mf.

People can bring about the tension and they can also relieve it. For example, this morning my kids brought about the stress, but they also took it away. Firstly, they kicked me all night in my bed, with the youngest having a screaming fit because he had a sore knee and ears.

Then they woke me at 7 am to begin the daily WWE at the kitchen table mixed in with a game of crystal maze. They said they wanted coco pops but what they actually meant was they wanted a yoghurt and to regurgitate cereal into a bowl for 20 minutes.

Once we got past this ritual the endless "I'm hungry" "I had that first" "I need that" began, all at a volume that could shatter glass. This was an endless circle of timeouts and complaints that reached the point where I felt like I could shoot myself just for 5 minutes of peace. Then something strange happened. They looked for the toys they liked, found them and played nicely. Not together, but nicely in the same room. 3 minutes of peace before the next argument but I'll take it.

It's just enough time for my patience level to return to just below roaring my head off feeling like a dragon all day. It's a sorry state when you dream of being ill so you can go to the hospital for a break.

I can tell when it's been a tough day for the kids as well as myself. They are pretty subtle and start answering my requests with "yes sir". The humorousness of their reply makes the guilt non apparent and acts as a small reminder to chill the fuck out. It's definitely needed most days, in fact I might just change my name to sir so that it feels like they sometimes acknowledge I am speaking.

Our happiest days have been filled with music. We listen to the same stuff all of the time and enjoy the comfort of familiarity, it makes us feel safe and calm. Familiar songs remind us of memories and specific moments or feelings in time and we get to relive all of those feelings again. Turns out this is a trauma reflex.
Surprised?
No, me neither.
What do you do though when you have a song that you love to bits because you can belt the words at the top of your lungs, but the song is connected with a bad memory? Does it make it more resounding when you're belting those lyrics out? Does the sound hit your soul more because of the feeling that returns or is just that it's a banging tune? I really don't know and I'm not sure I care because I will always interrupt someone talking to take on a power ballad.
No wonder I don't have many friends and the ones I do have are as fabulously brilliant as I am (also known as complete and utter fannys too.)

Do you ever just get random moments of anger? No rhyme or reason, just generally angry. Today I am angry at myself for getting sunburnt! I look like a lobster and what's worse is that I've burnt my bald head. Shame I don't tan or the bald might have blended into my hair. I can't wait until it starts peeling and I look like I have snow falling from my head.

I've had some amazing moments of happiness and sheer disbelief at the things that come out of my children's mouths. I'm not talking about the food that never reaches its destinations, but the sheer comical gold that expels from them (like a fart). For example the boys were playing a game of hide and seek (it never lasts long and does not involve a detective to find them, usually sitting under a blanket somewhere) and my eldest ran off to go and hide while my youngest shouts at me from his perch on the edge of the sofa like a little parrot " CLOSE MY EYES".

His hands are stretched out to the side, and I roar with laughter as I help him put his hands over his own eyes. Simple yet satisfyingly funny.

Other achievements this week included my eldest laying out 5 bundles of toilet roll to wipe his own ass and shouting to everyone in the household to come and revel in his triumph. The excitement in his voice made us run to him and then proceed to give him a round of applause before we hear a description of what his "jobby" looks like.

Obviously gross things happen all of the time living in a predominantly male household. There is at least one fart in the face, one willy joke and a bum wiggle on any given day (at least one of each minimum and I'm definitely underestimating).

We look at every type of bug there is at our disposal and usually try to take them home before I convince the boys that their families are right where we found the beastie and it needs to find its mummy. The good dinosaur is always a point of reference if I'm in need of a backup.

My crazy kids give lockdown a lot of meaning, in fact if it weren't for fear of them being ill, I would still be out working like some of my unfortunate colleagues who are cleaning what has already been cleaned and all productive tasks like such.

I have seen more people that remind me of normality recently. It's reassuring and a gentle reminder that life outside of the hell hole of 2020 does exist. Everyone I've spoken to seems to be on a similar page about it all. We want it to be over but not yet. We know it's far too early to begin reopening the gates of life, but the craving of normality teases us with everything we see.

We don't have it bad where we live. We can go for beautiful walks to the beaches, woodlands or countryside, we can also get anything we need either delivered by someone local or an online giant and we can contact whoever we need to (provided they want to answer their phones).

I have probably spoken to people more now than I would usually because of the expanse of time available. I only tend to have valuable conversations at the moment, mostly because I contact valuable people and they in turn contact me. It's a general nice feeling of love which becomes saddened by the fact we can't cuddle or hold our precious ones so dearly.

I miss hugging my nephews and my friends' children. I miss a warming embrace from my grandparents who were my safe zone. I would go to their house for an ultimate chill out time and to moan about everything and anything. I would settle for just getting to enjoy a cup of tea in the same room as them right now.

Death toll: 35,704
9 weeks in.

Kids are also developing Kawasaki disease at a more rapid rate than ever before, and no one can decide if it is linked to covid-19 or if it's a side effect of our fear induced generation. It's maybe just that we never reported this information before or maybe it's actually connected, but really no one knows. The whole country and possibly world is wandering around in a blind panic with no clue as to how anything works.
Our first minister in Scotland has been voted the best politician in dealing with the coronavirus. I feel proud that we are finally winning at something, although it's winning at losing against a deadly virus. In true Scottish style, even when we win, we lose.

Who do we have to blame?
 No one.
Literally, we have no idea who to pin all this year's gifts on apart from ourselves.

Control everything

This week has been the strangest thing ever. I don't know if it has been a week since I last wrote or whether it's been 2 days. It has been a week full of beautiful people and events. When I say beautiful people, I don't naturally mean externally, it's not the thing I notice. Actions and personality make someone beautiful.

Anyway, firstly our neighbour had a fall from a ladder after cutting his hedge. I didn't see the incident but came around the corner moments after. A few passers-by were calling an ambulance after seeing the amount of blood. In the moment of seeing how my neighbour was I grabbed some gloves, a mask and some first aid bits and bobs and headed over to his house where he had made his way indoors. I questioned myself before entering the house, given that I am at home shielding my sons, however I knew that my old neighbour and his wife were panicking, and I could help.

So, I go in and his wife is white as a sheet and totally panicked and I take a quick look at his head knowing paramedics are on route. It's a deep few cuts but we stop the bleeding and ask him a few questions before going outside to put away his tools. His wife was nervous, and her English wasn't great so when the ambulance arrived, they talked the ears off the help. The doc arrives at my house, and I am useless with pretty much all information as I didn`t see what happened. However, they manage to sort it all out and, in the end, he's doing grand and back out cutting his hedge the following day with a big ass bandage on his head. I'm pretty sure he's around 74 or 84, I can't quite remember but he's hard as nails.

His bravery and calmness in a panic of blood made me proud to know such a man.

Our neighbours have always been beautiful and kind, especially to our kids and I couldn't imagine seeing them hurt or in such a confusing situation, but these things happen on a daily basis.
We can't always prevent the hurt or awful situations we are put in, but the choice can be made to help or ignore.

The never-ending saga of 2020 continues, and we are now into week 10 of lockdown. It's depressing and sad in a lot of cases. Not having to stay at home to protect each other, but the idea of how we come out of this way of life without undoing all of the effort already put in. They are suggesting stages of kids returning to school including having marked out boxes in classrooms for designated areas for each child to stay within. Half home-school, half at school to keep classrooms small. Social distanced break times where the kids can be around each other and not touch, but only with their allocated group.

It sounds horrible and controlling. I don't want my child's first interaction with a building of education to be full of fear and panic. It's scary enough starting school, without being controlled in every aspect of your day. I don't particularly see how the system will work and I'm kind of writing it off as ridiculousness before it even begins.

The thought of it gives me the heebie jeebies (I can't believe that is actually a word according to the dictionary)

Anyway, we have had some other events this week, nothing of great importance but a lot of great hilarity. So, whilst out on our daily walk my kids and I go across the road to the playing fields at the academy. We were there for approximately 15 minutes and my eldest managed to fall once and my youngest twice (one of which bursting his nose open, the other creating a hole in his knee).

We decided to call it a day after my youngest also needs a pee but misses and soaks his trousers. Once we get home, we begin to get him stripped and find that he's wearing 2 pairs of pants. I'm dumbstruck and have no idea how this would even come about. He very rarely dresses himself so I know that it must have been me who put both pairs on him. WTF. I just kept thinking in my head, at least these can't be yesterday's pants because he had a bath this morning, or at least I think he did. What an Egg.

He's so adorable and innocent to even think anything is wrong with this and never thought to mention it.

My eldest has been acting a little strange and sensitive this week too and has had more frequent meltdowns than I can count. On one occasion he told me he wanted to make a bubble friend (like sponge bob SquarePants does) so that he would have a new friend.

This breaks my heart and I realise the impact this climate is having on a socialite like him. He's so friendly and outgoing, talks to anyone and literally just enjoys meeting new people, especially kids. This way of life is draining those skills from him, and he resorts to picking a few of his favourite teddies to be his new best friends. Screw corona in all its shiteness. We aren't even close to having the worst life even with this pandemic, but it sure still sucks for the kids.

I like my own space and quietness, but he obviously misses the interaction.

You would think that seeing familiar people would cheer them up, but I think without the physical touch it just doesn't quite count. We had a number of people come and visit (socially distanced, of course) and the kids seemed interested for approximately 5 minutes and then gave up and wanted to do other things. So, I am guessing the conversation part is great for adults but unless someone can play, it's just not the same.

I had a few days of feeling like crap again, just the usual covid cycle. It comes in phases and sometimes when you expect to have the world's worst day, it turns out to be a belter. Today for example, I barely slept after a million trips to get drinks for the mini gremlins, 1 pee-pee bed change and switching beds 3 times.

(Bed swap is a game that I like to play in the middle of the night and see how many different beds I can sleep in. I get extra points for being kicked or pissed on. Every night I score high, and I don't expect to lose anytime soon.)

The day went more amazingly than I could have imagined, so chilled, loads of happiness and smiles and lots of fun. We spent hours in the paddling pool and got an ice cream from the van which of course makes everyone happy. Before this we watched Sleeping Beauty and cuddled the kids which is probably the best way to start a day, feeling loved, relaxed and full of cereal.

We have had a few visits from a few people who don't mind coming to sit on the wall in the garden. We may all look ridiculous but it's probably less stressful than a normal visit to our home. A nice reminder of life before "the Rona" but not so overwhelming that we fear seeing others. I miss my friends and our families, but I also adore family time (this week) and feel like I am learning about my kids all over again.

I'm learning when to expect to cheek and when to let it go. I can trust my kids in particular situations as long as they aren't in the bathroom, or the cat isn't around. Rather than me chasing them around the house making sure they aren't in trouble, I'm trusting them to use what sense we have taught them (probably a really naive and stupid thing but we are about to start week 11 and the giving a fuck is not a constant in my life).

I had to explain my Thursday nights to my partner. We were brushing our teeth the other day and I let him know I was grumpy as a heads up warning for the day (we don't do telepathy in this house so best to use a different form of communication) and he queried whether he had done anything wrong, to which my reply was that I just needed a Thursday night. I miss my Thursday night moan with my work friends and the random stories that make you laugh until your sides hurt.

Nothing of any major significance has happened recently apart from seeing a ghost from the past. (You can tell there's a big story here, but I won't bore you with it.) A guy who used to be my step dad drove past my family when we were out for a walk.

Ok this sounds ridiculous, I might have to explain a little. He was a great guy kind of when he was with my mum, but things went sour when they split and then long story short, he married our next door neighbour, moved far away (hooray!), but recently moved back to the area.

He used to mean a lot to me, and I thought seeing him would be traumatic, but it just wasn't. It was like "oh there's that guy we haven't seen in ages" but not in the sense I would want to speak to him. It was more like seeing someone you knew from school but were not friends with. Long explanation to say basically nothing, I know.

It was the fact that I thought it would mean more to me and it didn't, but it must have meant something (or not) for me to write about it? Confused? Yes, me too.

On a note that's less confusing, a friend's brother contacted me the other day to send a gift of £50 to whoever or whatever we were supporting at the minute. (This makes me sound like I devote my life to charities and what not, but I don't, but we can't often see an opportunity to help go past us.)

So, I don't do more than what I expect of anyone else to do, but we love to give and help anyone that we can. This could be a simple gesture like my partner buying a skint neighbour a few things to see him by, or by sending money to a girl in south Africa who's supporting loads of families around them to eat during this crisis. (Which is something we had been talking about a lot on social media)

So, when I received this amazing donation, this is where we sent it along with a little extra because kindness inspires kindness. The feeling of having more than you need and being able to use it for someone else's benefit tells me that you are a kind person and have some pretty decent values in life.

You see suffering and you don't enjoy it, you then do what you can to try and help and sometimes that is enough. Thank you for being so kind.

I wanted to join this with what is happening in America right now, but I don't know how (I think I'm tired) because it's so crazy. A police officer knelt on a man's neck and killed him. He heard him beg for his life and he killed him for whatever reason, and he didn't take into account this man's life was at risk. Everything has kicked off and people are rioting, police cars are driving through crowds of protestors and using pepper spray like an air freshener. They are not being held responsible and I just don't even have the words for it.

George Floyd. (Who knew how this would age. Here's to change, Ching, Ching)

Estimated Death toll 37,460

Shit note to end on so here's a little perk to make this crazy world even more mad: on our bike ride the other day we saw a white rabbit hopping down the road. Not a word of a lie, I don't drink, I don't do drugs and my kids saw it too. I did suggest following him to find wonderland, but he was a fast fucker.

Dreamland is not funland

I had a dream last night that literally shook me. I woke up at about 5am unable to forget the dream or shake the fear.

Long and short of it, I killed one of my kids, or a child at least, but judging by the feelings that went along with the dream I'm guessing it was one of my own. It wasn't on purpose and happened in a car accident (once again). I don't quite remember the full dream, mostly the emotions that went with it.

After losing a child I did exactly what I thought it would and sunk away from life, skipping school and not going to work. Instead, I went to a different pool with someone from work (who I totally wouldn't expect) and swam there instead. On the way home I gave some of the most random people I know a lift while refusing to speak to them and having a permanent angry face.

The dream doesn't make a lot of sense and it's all a bit skewed in my memory, but I still woke up hating myself and the world. (that's pretty much how I went to sleep last night anyway. Thankfully it's still just a dream.)

The world is pretty shady right now, so I'm not surprised about weird dreams. Everyone is angry all of the time and there's a lot to be angry at. It's becoming a year of changes and information.

I would say truth, but that would be a massive lie. Encouraging people to tell the truth is sometimes an impossible feat, especially if they are under any form of stress or fear. It's happening across the globe and most of it is a long time coming, and some long overdue arrangements are sure to be set.

I feel it's a bit lost in this country, so although people are out protesting for freedom and the right to be treated equally, we have a government undercutting absolutely everything that would make the world a fair and more honest place. Instead, the country is out in masses spreading this virus that we have spent the past 3 months trying to subdue.

I believe so much that there needs to be so much change towards racism and how people of colour are perceived, I just don't agree with putting everyone at risk and that that is the only way to do it. We could be changing legislation, causing media blackouts to report only about what needs to be changed. When we are out of lockdown, we could feel the change and embrace a new way of life. Who am I to say any of this is true and appropriate either, I am just another opinion and probably not even a good one at that?

I'm frustrated after spending so long living away from the outside world and on multiple occasions today I have heard of people travelling hundreds of miles to visit others. I can't be the only one who gets frustrated seeing people who believe the rules don't apply to them. Fuck I even lived with one.

My partner at the start of lockdown woke up one day and informed me he was just going to nip to the dentist. I looked at him as if he had 3 heads and was speaking a foreign language. I then proceeded to projectile vomit a huge rant about him being the saviour of the world therefore the dentist would open just for him, and how they would possibly even have polished his throne in the waiting room for him.

He got it tight, in fact he still gets it tight. Until we received my youngest shielding letter, he was rather lax, and it bugged the shit out of me. This dafty has been the vent for all of my frustrations, unluckily for him, but I think he knows me a little better than before (we have been together 10 years so far, so you would think he would know it all) but it turns out you can always learn more about someone. Thank goodness because lockdown might have become extremely boring a long time ago.

He has become so trusting of me that he let me cut his curly locks, which he vowed to never let me do. I think the weight of his hair finally wore him down and he may have even started leaning to one side under the heavy stress.

Just kidding, but really, he looked like Tom Hanks when he starred in cast away and he needed the fresh haircut to boost his mood. We all know it, when you get your mush trimmed and you feel the dog's balls.

Anyway, I screwed up his fringe apparently and I felt the world of guilt, nail me as I saw the pure devastation in his face. He's not a ridiculously vain man, but he does like to look nice, and I on this occasion ballsed that up for a few weeks.

Fast forward a day and he doesn't think it's too bad, or at least that's what he's saying to save my feelings a little, although I couldn't hold back a stupid laugh when he looked in the mirror (guilt does strange things to you). I can take it, but I think he thinks I was taking the piss. I definitely wasn't but this reaction is normal in my family.

I grew up with a sister who laughed like an evil witch when she was scared. One example is of a camping trip we had at the bottom of Ben Nevis. We had been there a few days when late one night my mum had to go and sit in the car nearby to read a book, just so she could escape our ridiculous yapping (me and my two elder sisters who were teenagers at this point I believe).

Talking, (or probably arguing) in the tent we see this massive flame brighten up a whole side of our tent. The middle sister shouts fire and tries to head for the door out of the ten. I follow, however we are blocked by my eldest sister cackling her head off sitting in front of the zip of the door.

We finally manage to push past her and meet my mum outside the tent who is also in a state of panic. Our tent wasn't on fire (although it looked like it was going to be) and some guy that had camped up next to us had not set up his gas stove correctly, therefore set himself on fire and launched the flame ball in our direction. We emerged just in time to see the guy running through the camp side like a human torch towards the showers. He was ok and managed to not set himself on fire again for the rest of the trip.

Scared the shit out of us, but also highlighted who not to have in an emergency situation. (Well, when she was 13 anyway)

I'm not sure if camping has ever gone very well for us as a family to be honest. There have been multiple ridiculous situations that just don't even seem true.

First camping trip, a guy gets shot. My papa takes him and his mate to a payphone because he refuses to go to the hospital. (We went home after that and camped in the living room).

We went camping when there was hand, foot and mouth going about with the sheep and never knew (pre-social media days) We quickly left after the local shopkeeper warned us of a £1000 fine that we could receive.

Another camping trip with our neighbours I woke up in the middle of the night and told my mum something wasn't right, so we moved and slept in the car. No more than 5 minutes later our tent was crushed and wiped out by our neighbours tent and all the gas canisters and tables that were in it. It did create holidays that you wouldn't forget, but seriously something normal wouldn't go a miss. Maybe if it was normal, I wouldn't remember it.

I had to remember this was for my sanity. The past week or so has been dire. My mood has been draining and I am frustrated. The only thing that makes me happy consistently is the kids. They are hilarious and I'm assuming they get that from me.

Publicised Death toll 41,622

Be social, but dont

Life has begun to return to normal. Recently in Scotland we were allowed to meet with one other household outdoors, and now it's 2. You can use the toilet if you are at someone's house and more shops have opened. People have queued for miles outside of Primark to get their £1.50 flip flops for summer. I can't speak, I live by those cheap bargains and have a pair at home and work, different colours of course to match my ridiculous outfits. Who am I kidding, I never coordinate, luckily, I don't care?

I have begun watching a new series on Netflix when the kids go to bed called once upon a time. The CGI is terrible and the acting at times is sub-par, but the storyline and the actors are enchanting. The idea of living in a world where all of the Disney characters exist in our world and their stories follow them. It's a nice spin on actual reality, because the real world is exhausting.

I stopped listening to politics and pretty much the whole world. It's been peaceful and quiet, until people who care about me think I'm having a meltdown. Damn people giving a shit disturbing my peace.

Connection plays a part in all of our lives, some more than others and the depth of each connection can be overwhelming or hard to relate to. The one thing I cannot connect with is social media, mainly trying to decipher between fake news and actual loving life events from people.

I've literally seen a few baby announcements and a ridiculous meme that I have been able to even notice. There are a million ads for random crap we don't need, but because of the number of times we see them, we inevitably buy them. I now own oversized zorbees and a book of bingo cards to play with my friends over zoom. I'm yet to buy the wonder sports bra, but I'm sure if I see it flash up twice more, I'm going to buy it.

In a bigger size of course, because of the "Rona" I eat my body weight in bourbon biscuits every day.

The disconnect from the world becomes more prevalent every day and the desire to reintegrate into society is diminished. I've felt like this before maybe more than once, but mostly when I returned from a month long trip to

Ghana in Africa. The trip itself was voluntary working with a charity (village by village, give them a look up and you will be surprised) doing whatever we could to support the most rural villages of the growing country.

The lifestyle was so basic, not quite primitive but more of a survival. You didn't work your ass off to get a decent wage, you worked your ass off to get pennies and it was enough. It was enough to survive and provide for your family, sometimes.

Time didn't seem to exist at all. You can tell its daytime and night-time, but really apart from that, nothing. Say you ask someone to come and fix your car, he says he will be there around 1pm the next day. He actually arrives 2 days later at 7pm. This is Ghana time, and it's brilliant. Just don't ever make a schedule and expect it to be followed.

Coming back to this country from such a different plane of earth was horrible. I literally hated everyone for being so materialistic and busy. So many other things in life were more important than basic needs and kindness. I went to Tesco and planned to bargain with the cashier for a better price for my shopping, before remembering that wasn't socially acceptable. Woops.

In all seriousness I would love to live the life I did in Ghana in this country with the same climate. (Obviously the sun would help) no snakes though, you can keep those bad boys. We drove past 3 kids bludgeoning a massive snake to bits. They couldn't have been older than 8 years old, saving their own lives. I asked if we should stop to help, but who was I kidding, they were doing a much better job than any of us.

It was an experience of a lifetime and something I recommend for everyone and go alone. The experience will be more intense and fulfilling, well that's the idea anyway.

Today I had a conversation with my kids about asking what things were before picking it up. The item of interest of course was poop. Always.

Last night I had the worst night's sleep ever. I couldn't fall asleep because I sat and browsed stupid apps and when I did my youngest woke up wanting a cuddle. It's fabulous to be loved, but it's also great to get some sleep once every 5 years.

We cuddled in and then I had the worst nightmare I think I have ever had. It always happens between 4 and 5am. Last night began with a weird female stalker. She was supposed to be a teacher and would follow me around taking pictures of all the weirdest things you could imagine.

I managed to trap her when she tried to take a picture underneath a door and I stamped on her hand, pulled her arm in and held it while I grabbed her phone. I called the police and the situation seemed sorted and I can't remember if I let her go or not, but I thought the dream would end.

It didn't and I looked through her phone to find some strange messages about my eldest son. I immediately went to look for him and searched everywhere until I found an incinerator in the garden. Laid on the entry shelf was my son's bike, favourite teddy and blanket. I felt crushed.

I immediately knew what had happened and lost it. The actual feeling of being crushed from the inside was there taking over and leaving nothing but a howl from my soul. Instead of being able to change the dream, a million different scenarios were emerging.

The one that stuck was a small circular drain beneath my feet. Through the grate was my son's face with a hand over his mouth. The hand wasn't his and I had no idea what to do. I couldn't react or they would know I saw him. Once again, a million scenarios came into view of getting my child free. I woke up and have no idea how it ended. Again, sleep evades me because of my stupid brain, which incidentally is what needed sleep the most.

My partner got up with the kids and let me sleep a little. He woke me shortly after and proclaimed that we were climbing a hill and would be leaving very soon. Shit. I got up and was a mum. We climbed the hill, and it was beautiful and loving (as it could be with small kids).

At the top of that hill, we were even further away from the world than before. Happy kids enthralled in nature and adventure. We came home and went for a bike ride after a while. Then after dinner the most horrific rain came on. Surprise, surprise!

If it's sunny in Scotland, you know very quickly because it becomes like a day of worship.

The rest of the world is still screwed and as England has started to open up travel, we are becoming inundated with tourists. It would be great for the economy, however in Scotland there are still travel restrictions, so really none of it makes sense. We are no longer short of toilet rolls, but you can't buy a trampoline for love nor money and no one seems to really care for social distancing rules anymore.

Portrayed Death toll: 43,550 it's slowing but still growing.

TikTok takes over the world

I have avoided writing by complete accident for about 2 weeks, maybe more and I miss it, but I have had so many other projects I wanted to complete.

The last official days of nursery for my eldest were upon us very quickly and I had to make them as special as they should be. We still can't celebrate with his friends, but we did have an amazing day.
The nursery teachers had suggested a teddy bears picnic, to which my kids were delighted. Secretly so was I. I love doing things that are different and away from the norm, even just for a day to give you a sense of something. (I don't know what "something" is. I'm hoping inspiration on what it shall be, will return at any moment).

Anyway, visiting somewhere new and seeing something different is definitely largely welcome at this time. It currently feels like I'm on holiday for the summer and I sit and wait to see when I can return to work. We received a letter to tell us that our local GP would be reassessing all those on the shielding list.
It was relieving and worrying at the same time, we might actually have to reintegrate into society again (fuck that). It has been made worse by current family circumstances which I won't explain because it's absolutely ridiculous. Just trust me that the craziest things have happened this year and this could possibly be the topper. (How dare I leave out the juicy gossip)

Luckily, we distracted ourselves with a million arguments, scenic walks and eating lots of chocolate! Maybe not the best combination, but it worked for a while. It's like a plaster for an open fracture, but we're still trying and I'm sure that counts. The world is sinking and were building a rocket to get the fuck off it. (That wasn't supposed to be a poem)

The past week or maybe two (I'm kind of losing track of time) we have been isolating and totally distanced from the rest of our society. I don't think everything we do is completely correct, and I don't fully understand how I feel or what I believe in, but I think trusting my instincts is a pretty decent place to start.

On the plus side I finally managed to organise some life insurance for us both, only after I had a crippling nightmare about my partner dying. There were no play backs, retakes or fixing the situation. It just happened and I had to deal with it.

The dreams are becoming a bit debilitating and I'm so frustrated that I don't know how to fix anything in real life or dream land. We can't do anything, and it's so fucked up. I've lost touch with remembering funny moments with the kids and have spent a lot of time trying to bring them happiness and teach them things. This kind of works and they seem to enjoy life, but I can't remember what day it is most of the time and I'm only reminded that it's a new week because I see my grandparents again. The constant ones in life who always surprise me.

My friend messaged the other day and told me she was coming to town and was excited to see us and not going to lie. I could have cried with happiness at the thought of seeing someone familiar that I adore. It's all just a bit too bleak for now and unknown (and that has nothing to do with the ridiculous pandemic.)

It may be a real threat, or it could be a massive elaborate hoax, either way I don't care, and I don't want to pretend I do. I like my bubble as long as nothing can penetrate it.

We did meet up with one of my eldest's friends today and I got a yap with another mum who is as freaked out as me, maybe worse. I'm not sure but we agreed that we are nuts and are quite content in the fact that we at least know that about ourselves.

One thing that does cheer me up is the littlest chicken, if you have heard of him. It's a young guy on tik Tok who begins every video with "hiya pal, it's only me" before rambling about anything and everything. There's something about this wee guy and his tenants orange hat that makes him a joy to watch.

My other ray of sunshine is my work friend with the mad curly hair. She's great and without a doubt always makes me smile. She's an infectious fucker. I wrote this a week or so ago and sent this little snippet to her. She cried and it showed that voicing how much someone means to you, even with random profanity thrown in, can do.

I do genuinely mean she is amazing. She makes my heart smile all of the time, especially when I feel like the worst human alive. I wish for her all the happiness in the world and for those who surround her to be ones who appreciate her and understand her soul. I hope that you have been able to meet someone who does this for you. She is not the only one I have met in my life but she's definitely a Jem.

The past few weeks I have got a chance to meet up with many of my closest and kindest friends, and those I haven't met with I have spoken with on my phone. These people are the ones who keep you going. In the depths of what this shitty year has to offer, even seeing a picture of their happiness brings me joy.

Dancing in the rain

I miss the joy of life. It may sound crazy, but I miss simple joy and moments of contentment. These past few weeks have been so dark and unbelievable that an overwhelming sense of gloom and despair has lingered far too long. Too many issues unresolved and so much left unsaid. Also, too little time with those who mean a lot.

Today I cannot get out of my head. The thundering pounding rains. The day it rained so hard and fast you could barely see. The flooding began and it took me back to being a child. I love the sound of the rain, especially when it is pouring. I asked my kids if they fancied going outside and like I imagined they said yes. They are full of adventure and don't fear the weather of any storm. I hope this translates into real life problems when they grow, but for now puddle jumping will suffice.

We put on our crocs and went for it. (Yes, I own those ugly fuckers too, but I don't care about fashion, I'm more about function.) We hadn't even made it out the street and were surrounded by rivers running down the road. My youngest, who was previously too tired to walk, ran up and down numerous streets for the best part of an hour finding the biggest puddles to jump in. The whole time we did nothing but smile and revel in the gift that nature had delivered. We eventually only gave up and came home because the rain stopped, and the drain began to cope with the immense volume of water. It will forever be one of my happiest moments in life with my kids. I have so many, but this one is in with the greats. Maximum happiness and laughter for all of us.

We seemed to have a good run of these moments with a couple of days exploring. My partner suggested a walk which he had done before with work for us, however we never realised that half of the path down a steep hill had been washed away. We went through the jungle of overgrown fern and nettles, down a muddy narrow route to reach a beach. (Not just any beach, a beach called Sunnyside) It was secluded and beautiful in every sense of the word. Walking down off the hill to grasp a view of the place was magical and left me awestruck.

I thanked him greatly for leading us to such amazement and we finished our visit to this part with a picnic on the rocks and playing in the sea. Before we got back to the car there was a castle to explore.

We never realised how treacherous this visit to the castle could be until we were there. The sheer drops of either side of the narrow path were unbelievable and once you entered the castle you had to grip the walls to prevent yourself from slipping out the windows (or what used to be windows as they were now gaping holes in the wall).

My kids revelled in the delight of the journey and my partner, and I tried to hide our panic and fear of losing grip of their hands. I thought I was scared, but really it felt like nothing when I looked into my partner's eyes. It was as if he was being forced to confront his worst fears all at once. That's when I realised that I wasn't actually overreacting, it was genuinely terrifying. If it had been a dryer day and not so many mudslides, I imagine it may have been different. None the less the whole experience was invigorating. We went home and enjoyed the comfort of our home whilst yearning for adventure.

The following day we opted for a less dangerous route however we met where we had been the day before from the other side. (Did that make sense, it did in my head, but I can see what I mean. I was about to explain that it was a coastal walk, but if it's a beach we visited then where else would it be?).

We also got to have another packed lunch on some rocks not far from our previous lunch spot and watch some rock climbers tackling some really good looking stacks. It felt like a dreamworld that didn't really exist. You know that feeling you get when you go on holiday abroad and it's mesmerising, and you feel a million miles away from the world and its awfulness.
That was it.
Sitting with my bag of crisps and apples watching those climbers was my holiday for the year and I'll take it. It was possibly more reassuring because I knew when I got back to my car, I was only a fifteen minute drive away from home.

This week has brought a few enlightenments for our future, well this next month anyway. My youngest got an x-ray of his leg which came back completely normal as expected. It's ridiculous to say I was disappointed, but I was. I wanted there to be a clear cut reason as to why he was in so much pain walking for any length of time, but I think I also wanted to know if this wasn't in my head.

He loves to run and be active but when he pushes himself too far, he suffers and feels pain at all times of the day, or so he tells me. I keep thinking, could this be an elaborate hoax from him so that he doesn't need to walk everywhere or is this genuinely a probable cause for concern. I actually don't know anymore, but I can't just assume he's at it, or can I? I genuinely don't know about anything anymore.

This year has thrown my internal compass off balance, it doesn't know and neither do I. I don't want to let self-doubt and guessing games take over, but I do feel like I'm fumbling around in the dark trying to find a light switch in a maze. Oh, and the maze is on fire and spinning at a million miles an hour. 2020 in a nutshell.

Death toll data: unreliable.

All sources of collecting such data are a joke. Apparently, you can get hit by a bus and Covid-19 would be put on your death certificate, so unfortunately at the end of all this we don't know the official damage that has been caused because everything is actually a lie, and that's true.

EUGH

I also received a phone call from my boss this week saying that I was to return to work as the Scottish government was now lifting shielding restrictions. Yay! Not. I love my work, but the place also gives me a million reasons to hate it. I could actually use that phrase to discuss almost anything in the world right now and it makes complete and utter sense to more than just me. I don't know how I feel about returning, however one of my bosses who has worked there for years has quit, which does not exactly give me a sense of reassurance that all is well.

I am gutted for this boss to be leaving because they were one of the ones who actually tried to protect the staff. If I needed an answer, I would go to them and I would get it, or I would at least find some form of resolution. They could be rather moody at work, but if you knew the circumstance, you could more than empathise. In fact, I couldn't count how many times I was grateful I didn't have their job. I genuinely think that for them to gain any form of peace and satisfaction, the best thing was to leave that job. I genuinely hope life is so much more pleasant for them, but for filling their role, I have no idea what will happen.

I don't want to make my work seem like an awful place because in essence it's not, it's lovely most of the time. However, it's scary to think about returning there when I can't even take my own kids to a playpark. We've literally only just been allowed to enter someone else's home, for the first time in 4 months, today. It's all happening rather fast for how slowly it was all shut down. Everyone is expected to return to normal life and be ok about it, as if we haven't just dealt with a 4 month seclusion from society.

Most commonly used phrase this month: I don't know.

Most common thought this month: Fuck this.

What's in the news: dinosaur embryos, and elite pedo rings.

If you are just joining us, welcome to the shit storm that is 2020 and may the odds be ever in your favour.

Find me at the beach, always

So yesterday we went to the beach in the pouring rain, because really what does it matter if it's raining or sunshine when you're at the beach.

It was supposed to be a beautiful day, but of course because we had planned to spend all day there it was going to rain. I was pleasantly surprised by the amount of sea creatures we found. We went armed with buckets and spades and caught about 18 little crabs and 1 starfish who looked like he was regrowing a leg. 2020 must have been a tough year for him too.

It was all going so well until the last rockpool where we had already caught about 5 crabs in and as we were about to pull another, something moved beneath my foot. I moved a little and out comes this massive fucker of a crab. I of course freaked out as I was in my bare feet, which in turn confused the kids. They stood and laughed at me as my partner ran a mile. His thoughts were evidently the same as mine. Time to go home.

Beach finds have sometimes been the highlight of our days. Yesterday it was lobster tails and golf balls. My mum collected an array of things and took them home and gave a list of what to do with it all. Circle shells make excellent necklaces.

I think the beach is just something I'm not sure I could live without anymore.

Do one Daisy

I've spent a few weeks questioning my perspective. The idea that whatever perspective we have is the appropriate one for our lives. Also, how many things can alter our perspective and make it skewed, or less so. It's one of those questions that if you delve too deep, your head ends up in a knot.

Maybe the best idea is to go with what you immediately within yourself understand is best, until something occurs that makes you believe otherwise. I'm not sure. Everything is questionable. (I mentioned this to one of my work friends the other day and she looked as if I had grown 3 heads. She then asked me to repeat what I said in layman's terms. It did lead to an interesting conversation after I stopped speaking in riddles).

The unknown seems to be the most interesting subject, however also the most terrifying at times.

I also went back to work this week and it was worrying. In Fact, a little bit more than worrying. The night before I was due back, I couldn't fall asleep. My head sat in a tailspin of what was going to happen. How many uncomfortable situations was I going to be put in? what was I going to be expected to do that I hadn't done for months. I literally couldn't slow my brain down and I felt like my heart was pounding but my watch told me otherwise.

I had no idea how to stop it or control it, but I just wanted to sleep. Eventually the sleep thief (aka my youngest son) climbed into my bed and a snuggle with him made dreamland that little bit easier to reach thankfully.

The shift wasn't even that bad once it arrived. The building isn't open, and staff are not doing a lot of anything, mainly because there's not a lot to do. It was nice to see people again, but I'm not completely sure I couldn't survive a little longer in isolation.

The following day I was working again, however I managed to sleep a little better at night and I thought I had immediately gotten over the fear of work. This was until I got the nervous shits before leaving.

Fear rears its ugly head in different ways. It's as if it's just trying to surprise me and keep my life interesting.
I appreciate the effort, in fact no I don't, that's a lie. I do wish it would kindly fuck off.

Death toll 46,201. Maybe

Celebrate it all

So, the more often I was at work, I assumed that I would feel more and more at ease. This wasn't the case and I seem to become more and more tense. If I am working an early shift this becomes more apparent in the lack of sleep, though not actually being able to switch off and having constant battles with myself about what should be happening. What is safe to do and essentially how long is it before we eventually contract this virus.

I had this image in my head I couldn't shake and every argument I was prepared to have led right back to this same scenario. The hospital room where my son was curled up into a ball to have a rather large needle pierced into his spine to gather some cerebral fluid.

(Warning: Long winded explanation in here, the significance is there I think)

Now I wasn't in the room the first time this happened, however the second time I refused to leave. I had to sit in a faraway corner and not touch my child. Luckily, (if that's what you can call it) he was almost unaware of what was happening because his little tired out body couldn't keep him awake anymore.

Whatever had infected his body was literally taking everything he had left. I felt sorry for the doctor performing the procedure with me watching. I did ask if she would prefer, I left the room, if it would give her more focus and less nerves, however she assured me that she was quite happy for me to be there and was more worried about me not coping.

The procedure was going well and as the needle punctured my child's spine, the fluid that is supposed to drip out, sprayed with such intensity that it hit the wall behind the doctor. She never flinched and said as calmly as ever that it was such a strange thing to happen, and that this poor child had one hell of a headache with that kind of build-up in pressure.

This little scenario is something I do not ever want to repeat. At the time, it was so important for me to have as much information as possible, and I was in awe of what the doctor and her magical hands were doing that I found it fascinating.

Doctors will generally always be superheroes in my eyes, unless of course you get the odd arsehole, but most of them are not bad. Medical staff in general are something of a wonder due to the amount of information they must hold within their brains. If I had the nerve, I would have loved to be a doctor. I would also need the brains to go along with it so I'm not sure where I would acquire that. I'm probably best sticking to my day job.

Funny things are sometimes hard to spot in daily life at the moment, however I did have an extremely proud moment. My eldest son had his first playdate without me. He went to a friend's house (who he literally adores) and asked that I not go with him. As he left my front door on his little adventure, I was ridiculously proud.

The confident little guy that is wandering along the street with his friend and her mum didn't even need to look back for reassurance. He came home with glowing reviews of his behaviour and mentioned to me that he had done a pardon (a burp) and had forgotten to excuse himself. He knew the difference between what was okay in our home and how to behave outside. Most definitely an achievement in my books.

Celebrate everything and anything you can. No matter how small the achievement.

My youngest however spent the first hour with his sad face on because he missed his brother so much. Also, an achievement? Yes. he loves his brother (when he's gone)

We also had another first this week, something I never expected to be doing with my kids especially at 5 and 2. We left the house and went for a picnic in a nearby town when my partner decided we should check out all the old "jumping in" spots he used to do with his brothers.

It was beautiful and of course a bit of rock climbing was involved but once we arrived my partner decided to take his top off and launch himself in the North Sea. This was common when we were 14 when we were a lot less fearless.

There was a considerable amount of deliberation before he jumped (showing his age) but when he did the kids were amazed. My youngest decided that he wanted a go too. Stripped to his pants and sandals and jumped with his dad.

I honestly was so proud of him, showing no fear. Usually, he's the kid who moans and needs to be carried or dragged along, (kicking and screaming of course) but not with this. Turns out the kid is a weapon and is definitely going to cause me some trouble for years to come.

We returned to the same spot today, this time more equipped for the event and went on a little adventure round the coast jumping in the freezing water and swimming with the kids on our backs. To be honest it felt a bit ridiculous at times and I kept thinking "imagine we get stuck or something stupid and have to call the chopper" fucking tits.

Then the sea water splashes, and the idea of a new adventure takes over and I'm in love with our choice of activity for the day.

The only downside was having to get stripped roadside to get changed but really that wasn't even much of a bummer because of the cracking sunshine melting all day. A good day to be in Scotland.

Happiness exists for a few days! I did swallow some sea water so I can't wait to feel the effects of that!

You would honestly think between nervous poops and deliberating wearing a nappy to save climbing the stairs so much to poop, that I might have actually lost a wee bit of weight.

I'm missing my long friends (the ones who live forever away) and would love to just meet up for a few days. I usually can't deal with leaving them again so it's not always the best idea but is always worth it.

The last time I visited my friend in Sheffield it was amazing. However, after leaving I didn't stop crying until I reached Carlisle. Even then I only stopped because we had to go to Tesco and get something to eat. (I looked like I had just been abused because of the bags under my eyes).

It sounds ridiculous and a bit over the top, but this friend in particular was referred to as my replacement boyfriend for a while (also over the top, she was the best friend). This was because I spent more time with her than I did my partner, I owe her so much. The annoying part is that I can do almost nothing for her living hundreds of miles away. She used to be there for everything, including the whole of my first pregnancy, and I so wish I could have done for her what she did for me. She has this handsome little boy who I just adore and wish I could spend my days with.

Also, her family are actually just brilliant, literally just lovely and so entertaining. When she lived with her mum and dog, they used to wander around the house not talking to each other but talking through the dog. It was the "Millie voice" so essentially, they had this sassy ass dog who they would imitate as if she could participate in conversations.

The most ridiculous part was they must have done this so much because their voices were in exact synchro and sounded identical.

We live in parallel universes at times, and I so despise the world being so big.

My other long friend doesn't actually live that far away, but also has 2 children which makes life just that little bit harder.

Lockdown and the Rona have actually given us a chance to make time for each other. We had weekly quiz sessions (primary age quizzes because we are thick as fuck) with a prize for the winner for a while and it was usually the highlight of my week.

One of these friends is someone who never imagined herself having kids, ever. In fact, when my eldest was born she refused to hold him until he was thrust into her arms when he was about 8 months old. She surprised herself, I think and had 2 beautiful kids that she can move mountains for.

I love my girls ridiculously and adore their kids even more than I could have ever imagined and today I really miss them. (Can you tell?)

Don't doubt yourself

So many people have so many different ideas in the world and even tiny little details of information can be totally skewed depending on the source or how much attention the recipient is paying. The world seems to live in a game of Chinese whispers.

Also depending on individuals reactions to particular moments can give a positive or negative view. In essence the world is full of the unknown and the greatest variable is the human race. What's ridiculous is humans as a race cannot be classified to have common characteristics in behaviour and they certainly cannot be classed to be a group who support each other but are more like spiders or sharks.

Maybe we are supposed to live alone to protect others in the world. When we see other humans, we cannot help but encourage destruction within each other.

Anyway, back to real life. Something tragic and rather unexpected happened in our country today. There was not a massive loss of life or great deal of injuries however the country or maybe even just the shire were rather shook.

A train derailed after a landslide. The heavy rain from the day before flooded streets and washed the land away causing this early morning train to derail. 3 men died, 2 of whom worked on the train. 6 more people were injured. It doesn't sound like much however considering there were only 14 people on the train reminds us of how much devastation there could have been.

The thunderstorms of Wednesday the 12th of August felt like a bit of a bad omen. Everyone awoke to the flashing of lightning and growls of thunder. I awoke and felt like the world had angered the gods. Our country was sending the kids back to school that day.

I had pictured my son's first day of school all teary eyed, waving goodbye with gleaming smiles of pride. I also worried that he would be howling at the door screaming "mum" as they dragged him in the door, however being optimistic I didn't dwell on the latter situation too much.

9 am came and the rain began to slow. Luckily because of "the Rona" primary 1 kids didn't start until 9:30 am. By 20 past 9 the sunshine had arrived and had already begun drying the streets. 9:30am came and I got to wave goodbye to my eldest son as the sun was blazing down, all the kids had smiles on their faces, and it was like a dream. I couldn't imagine the first day of school beginning more perfectly.

Bad omen? Possibly the universe is trying to make us doubt ourselves, making sure we don't feel too comfortable returning to some form of normal.

My partner has had a tough few weeks, possibly months and usually I spend my time trying to annoy him as much as he annoys me. For a change, I gave him a break. Mostly because I didn't have the energy to be a dick and I think he was grateful. He even offered and volunteered himself to do some DIY in the house. (This is the same man whom I recently taught how to hang a picture frame)
I am so very grateful for him this week.

I've seen a lot of keyboard warriors this week, well for the past few weeks complaining about everything and anything they possibly can, and I can't decide why these people have become so invested in spreading fear and hate as often as they can.
Most complaints come from wearing a mask in shops and how it is the government just trying to control us.

Could there be more important things to moan about?
What I would like a solution for is how to stop my kids from licking everything in sight. That would possibly be an ideal solution to stop the spread of covid.
The effect this deadly virus has had on the world and economy is exponential and the actual deadliness of it is questionable, however if we spent a little more time trying to take down the elite paedophile rings rather than moaning about wearing a mask, we may be a little more successful.
Just an opinion, again and probably still not the right one.

Anyway, the first week of school was over (which lasted 3 days) and we are enjoying the weekend of relaxation and sunshine. We went to the beach today before dinner for a quick stroll and to play in the waves and I thought it would be glorious. Oh, how wrong I was.

The kids enjoyed themselves and had so much fun and we found a really big (dead) crab on the shoreline. For a change I had also brought my dog along because the beach wasn't too busy, but this was to be a grave mistake. He adores the water so I let him off his lead to run around and enjoy himself too, but he decided that this crab would be fun to play fetch with. Cue me running around trying to get him to drop it, just in case it was still alive (also a mistake), and he comes charging at me with the claws hanging out his mouth to give to me to throw. I run away, which of course encourages him to run faster towards me. He eventually drops this poor thing in the water and dismembers it.

Enough is enough I decide it's time to leave the beach and the kids start heading towards the ramp to the grass. The dog stands still. Refusing to move I stand torn in what to chase. Do I go after the kids and leave the dog before I lose sight of them, or do I try and wrangle the arsehole out of the water? I of course go after the kids.
The dog follows for a while before bolting back to the sea. I find the kids and tell them they need to come with me to get the dog to which they oblige (for a change). The dog by this point has come out of the water again and has decided to pee on a stranger's bag on the beach. Yas! It just gets better.

I finally manage to encourage the dog to come back to get his lead on by making sounds as if I'm going to be sick. Apparently, this is his new recall sign. I look like an absolute dick stranding on the beach shoeless, wet, covered in sand and making sick noises as a colleague comes past and asks "how's it going?" I replied "Grand thanks!" before returning to my vomiting noises. Did I mention my kids are wearing nothing but pants and are also covered head to toe in sand?

When you try to do something nice for someone and they piss on your face. Well, a stranger's belongings in this case. (Luckily it was some very understanding young girls and their stuff did not appear to be damaged thankfully). I have spent the rest of my night cursing the arsehole of a dog I have and will no longer take him to the beach to be unleashed!

Also, here I am considering getting a new pet to add to our clan. Will it be a wise decision, probably not? Will I still do it? Of course.

I got to come home to my kids and enjoy our home at least. Our newly decorated home. I decided the other day that I didn't have much to do and could scroll Facebook all night so it would freshen up our kitchen. I received a tin of paint from our neighbours because they didn't like the colour and knew how much I enjoy painting.

I laid out some lines on the wall with masking tape and stripped to my underwear because I'm too lazy to climb the stairs for my painting clothes. I did go upstairs for multiple paintbrushes and painting trays, but it never once occurred to me I should put on any clothing. Luckily my kitchen window looks into my back garden and none of my neighbours can see in the window (well I hope they can't).

I painted and finished within an hour much to my disgust as I would have to find something else to fill my time with, but I felt accomplished. Something that is almost impossible to feel within my current work life, but I can achieve so many times at home.

My grandma also fell ill recently and ended up going to the hospital for a day, unfortunately because the local hospital is an hour away and that city is in a lockdown because of a surge in cases, she had to go alone. My grandparents are very rarely apart, so for my Papa this was surreal, and he hated not being able to be with her.

The lockdown re-occurred because pubs were one of the businesses that could reopen and as soon as people could they flocked to the pubs like flies on shit. Unfortunately, none of them bothered to use common sense and protect themselves in any way or social distance, therefore the city went into lockdown because of the number of close contacts affected within days of a night out.

We are still yet to figure out why pubs were reopened before the kids could return to school. In Fact, I can't even join my son for his school lunch experience because of covid, but I can go to a pub or restaurant and have lunch with anyone else. My son will luckily not know the difference, but I do, and I know what we are missing out on. I took holidays from my work so that I could join him as part of his first year in school, but I guess the young team getting to have a social life is more important than a 5 year old getting to feel safe and supported through life.

Probably a bit dramatic but I'm pissed off.

If I haven't said this before fuck covid and the shitstorm that it has caused. Fuck 2020 and the people in the world who have caused the most unthinkable things to happen this year.

P.S. I don't get to swear at home around the kids and at work it's inappropriate but here I get to call out the arseholes and wankers of the world.

Ray of sunshine

Do you ever have a day when you don't want to participate in the world? Like not enough to not want to be here at all, but definitely avoid the whole rest of society.

Life is returning to normal mostly. You still have to wear a mask entering most places and travelling any distance is still a rather taboo subject. (Not that this stops anyone)
I can't actually criticise anyone because of a trip I took to meet my new-born niece. It wouldn't have been so bad, but it was literally the length of the country. 10hrs driving to spend 3 hours there and then 10 hours to get home. Driving time wasn't exactly that long due to a decent turbo diesel engine. However, a grand total of 1120 miles in 24 hours, but boy was she worth it. The first girl born into the family of her generation and an amazing ray of hope for a really crap year.
I couldn't help but apologise to her as I held her tiny hands. Apologising for the shitty world she was brought into and sorry for being grateful that she is in this terrible year just so that we get to meet her. How ridiculous I know. It was a stressful journey that took all of my will to go on.
My dad was driving, and I had to just get to his house which is an hour away from mine. I took my elder sister through too but couldn't shake this horrible feeling. I was ready to take her through and drop her off and come home. I felt this way until I entered my sister's home and saw my niece. Even standing outside the door, 10 hours away from my own home I still thought "it's not too late to turn back"

Is there anything that I haven't written recently that hasn't been ridiculous? Probably not and what's worse is that I don't put in the craziest stuff that actually goes on. I save you all from that whole pile of hairy shit.

My work is starting to fill up again with customers and swimming pools are now opening, which is great apart from having more work to do and less people to do it with. It's not a fun or pleasant job anymore because your feet usually swell up like balloons from running around like a headless chicken or you smell like a mouldy tea bag from sweating your balls off all day.

Talking to people is also not that fun anymore as what they tend to want is information on the latest operational updates and 9 times out of 10, they know more than I do. I have apologised for giving false information more this week than I've had cups of tea. It's not a great ratio to have, but still, I cannot and should not complain about having a job.

There's been another rise in cases (probably because you can now get tested and there's this fancy thing called track and trace, meaning other people get contacted to be tested too) meaning that we can no longer meet up with more than 2 households and at a maximum of 6 people at a time. The exception to this is if you are going to work, school, pub, supermarket, cinema, gym or to play football. Makes sense that all of these essential things are on the same list.

It was pointed out to me today that I can go to work and then to school to collect my kids (where they spend time with up to 20 other households at least) , but I can't walk home with more than 1 other household or go to more than 1 persons home, but I can take the kids to football, and go out for dinner. I can then also pop into the gym to profusely sweat over 12 other people too before nipping for a pint, but I shouldn't have my grandparents and mum round at the same time or chance facing a fine. Makes sense.

Oh, and also whilst you are walking around socially distanced from everyone, you must wear a mask, but when you're sweating and jumping about or if you just don't fancy it, it's all good to leave that fucker at home.

Backwards knees are the only thing I can think of to describe this fuckery.

This way of living either drives you into severe loneliness and anxiety or it sends you into a treat mode, where you literally say yes to as much as you can. Movie night and popcorn for the 5th time this week? Hell yes. Pizza again? Yes. giving up your job and working from home with no idea about business? Why fucking not.

I haven't exactly done any of this, but the idea of being at home all the time and just being in love with my kids and having a content life really makes me want to quit my stable job. I have always been a bit of a hermit and enjoy my own space with my crazy ass thoughts, probably because that way no one can judge you. You are your own judge and jury which generally works well for your mental health unless you are not of sound mind in the first place, or you have to re-join society.

There doesn't seem to be an ending to this way of living, and I don't think there is a way back. It's not the worst thing that people wash their hands more often or that personal space has become a thing again, but when a close friend hugs your child on the street out of sheer joy and delight in seeing them and then feels the need to profusely apologise, then I begin to wonder if we have gone too far.

I still fear for my kids becoming ill or not coping with a deadly virus, however I don't feel the need to deprive them of relationships and love in life. I cannot prevent them from getting sick, in fact my youngest has fallen and been hurt accidentally so much in the past week that I fear we may be contacted by social services. I blame it on his adventurous side and the desire to squeeze himself between every wall and lamppost on the school run. Also, you can tell this boy that something is dangerous and will hurt him a million times and he will still go and do it.

The purpose of me as a mum is to be there to clean the wounds and mend the heartaches, whilst trying and failing miserably to prevent them in the first place.

I recently had a movie night 2 nights in a row with my curly reception friend. The second night was to recover from the trauma of the first night's movie. We watched a movie on Netflix called Cuties and were completely horrified.

Do you ever remember watching terrible movies in school that highlighted and over exaggerated all the things in life that you shouldn't do? (Like a creepy junkie offering heroin to a 12 year old, or an old man dressed as Willy Wonka inviting you into his car.) It was one of those.

Everything seemed exaggerated to the point of making your skin crawl and your soul literally trying to claw its way out of your body. 12 and 13 year old girls dancing half naked, sexually to be part of a dance competition. It seemed surreal watching it with close ups of these kids unmentionables at every opportunity, mixed in with some racial polygamy mixed in too. Once the movie was finished, we googled the ages of the actresses to find that they are actually only 11/12 years old in real life too. Their parents and a full movie crew watched these scenes being filmed and not one person thought that the movie was becoming rather inappropriate.

The whole idea of the movie is to show the modern world and what our children are brought up to believe is ok, I get it, it's there to make you feel uncomfortable. However, did we really need a movie about inappropriate behaviour to highlight how much inappropriate behaviour is going on in the world? It's like committing a crime to show why the crime is bad.

Anyway, we watched trolls world tour the second night to lighten our newly blackened souls, however was rudely interrupted by this massive fuck of spider. My heart rate peaked for the day for a full 30 minutes and we rearranged the living room to find this thing. My great friend decided that throwing a glass at the spider would be more effective than placing it over the top of it (possibly why it took 30 minutes to get rid of it). The spider was finally caught by a friend passing by my house that was flagged from the window to come and help the idiots in distress. He quickly caught the spider in a tissue and wandered out the front door again saying "have a nice night" in about a minute. Anti-climax or what?

You know when you read a book and then it just ends. Not a normal book, but one that you are deeply engrossed in and enfolded in all the characters and then it ends. That was what happened that night and to be honest I'm not sure if I've even recovered now, almost a week on.

I have, however, in an attempt to spider proof my house, sprayed diluted vinegar on every surface possible until I can get more conkers to keep the awful things at bay. It also helps keep visitors at bay, because the new stench makes your eyes water as soon as you walk through the door. I will do anything to be beastie free all year. In Fact, in my last home, I had attempted to make a sign small enough for spiders to read to place at the front door as a warning to the intruders. I changed my mind after believing that they probably didn't speak English let alone read, but you never know. Once again, I will try anything.

Life felt like it was returning to its normal exhausting state before the government then decided that it might need to impose a lockdown again. The difference this time however is that people are totally over the whole situation. No one really believes that covid 19 is as scary and ridiculous as they have made it seem. There are still a few people who fear for life and stick to restrictions beyond current guidelines, but most people are fed up with not having actual connections in life and want to return to the world.

I personally like my little bubble but returning to only having 2 households in one place seems beyond belief. I don't feel like we are at more of a threat from covid-19 as we are from the common cold. It's probably something that we are going to have to integrate into normal life unless they plan to shut down my work again, I don't particularly see the need for drastic measures.

I began thinking today about social media and the effect it has on our lives after hearing about a documentary that was made about the detrimental advances it now poses on humans. I know I personally feel exhausted if I talk to too many people in a day, but could this be because of the interaction I have on social media?

Does it make a difference in conversations if you have spent a portion of your day already involved in other people's lives online to actually having to converse on a face to face basis.

Like do you reach the point of hearing enough about other people due to social media that you cannot bear to think about anyone else? Quite possibly. I know I spend most of my time on my phone watching videos on life hacks and craft ideas rather than flicking through Facebook posts and even then, if I have seen something created in a video, I no longer feel the need to carry it out. Does it also hinder the need for imagination? You can no longer be creative due to watching so many other ideas being brought to fruition. I'm not sure, but it's definitely something worth looking into.

The definition of fact and fiction has also become almost indistinguishable. Depending on what you see on a daily basis, decide your actions for the future. Not even possibly that far into the future. Daily tasks and life decisions can be based on your emotions of that day depending on what you have seen the night before and most of the time is from whatever is in your news feed.

Conspiracy theories are fast becoming part of daily conversations due to what we are being exposed to. Identity has almost disappeared and in most cases, no one knows what is going on. In Fact, I've thought it myself multiple times, especially over the past year. Which in turn leads to a major increase in mental health problems. Our brains aren't being taught how to deal with actual life, because truth doesn't exist, fear is exponentially forced upon our daily lives by simple ideas that are planted in adverts and random social media posts.

The worst thing I have witnessed from this is people trying to expose all of the threats of the world, telling us that the world is lying to us. Which of course is a fine opinion to have until it comes to the point of abuse for not believing in what someone else believes.

If you wear a mask you are a sheep. If you, don't you are enlightened. Enlightened to ideas that aren't even yours and are no more confirmed than facts that come from any other source.

It used to be that you trust what makes sense to you and what you believe to be more than plausible. However how can that be true any longer if information (fact or fiction) is being forced into your life through every avenue possible. You are made to believe what the outside work makes you believe. It makes free will seem like a thing of the past and we haven't even realised it yet. Who do you believe? What sources do you count as honest and viable? And why?

One step forward

Our leader for this country has introduced more restrictions recently which has taken us a leap backwards. More and more people are against it, and I have struggled with it myself. I can't have anyone in my home again, but am I really able to give up this luxury again? Yes.

The decision for me has been my partner having a covid test. It was a test that also looked for antibodies to the virus. I really had been hoping that he would test positive, and we would have had Covid-19 and never knew about it but were somewhat immune. Now I am basing this decision on a test that I believe to be true. Am I wrong for this? Possibly, depending on where your beliefs sit.

Being a manipulative person is classed as a terrible trait to have, so why are we so happy with using computer programming that is focused on manipulation? (Aka book face)

We have had a lot of fun the past few weeks, but time has really flown past. We managed to go conker hunting, collecting hundreds of course to keep the spiders at bay for another year hopefully.
We also began harvesting our sunflowers, which is a completely new experience for us. My son took one to school (with a note asking if he was allowed due to the pandemic, of course) and his teacher spoke to me at the end of the day completely delighted by this sunflower head and had sent my son to the next class to show them also. He got a sticker for his achievement and was filled with pride when I picked him up. I couldn't have been happier for him. He also went to school today with a bundle of plasters in his pocket that he told me he needed in case anyone got hurt in the playground.

Proud mum today at his sheer delight and thought processes. He can be so ridiculously kind and then come home and dive bomb me on the sofa with a karate chop to the face. It's all about balance.

Another announcement, another step backwards. This time it's detrimental for pubs and restaurants. Alcohol is the demon that some can't live without, however now they will have to after 6pm. So much for "go hard or go home". If you want to go hard you better go home because the boss said so. Oh, and do it on your own because you can't have any visitors. Tough one to take if you don't have anything else in your life at the minute.

Is the first minister indivertibly teaching people to crave for more in life? Something other than a drink and nothingness. She's removing all of the distractions that usually keep us going and avoiding our problems. No wonder mental health rates have blown up, for the first time in forever people are having to slow down and look at themselves. This obviously isn't the only reason for it, but definitely part of it.

Lines are blurring

We haven't really moved on from this stage. We are now in November and for about the past 2 months things have not changed on a national scale. England entered another lockdown and Scotland began using a tier system. Level 1 is almost normality, level 4 is full lockdown apart from schools.

This is great apart from the constant moaning from every direction, about anything and everyone. I am guilty of this myself and really think I want another break. I want a break from family, friends and work just to be alone in my home with my kids and partner. This is possibly just a feeling I have had this week (as it's been a tough one) but really, it's been brewing for a while.

The most recent kicker was my brother. He crashed his car and got hurt really bad. He broke his back and somehow survived after being catapulted from his car at 70mph. I don't know how, but he's alive. The whole week was spent being worried that he wouldn't be ok, that somehow the doctors missed something, and he wouldn't be ok. He's my little brother and I still feel like he should be 12, but he's almost 18 and is proving himself to be the beginnings of a great man. (Not that I can tell him this, as his head wouldn't fit through doors)

I don't know how my dad, or his mum will ever really cope with this experience as it's been dramatically worse in the middle of a pandemic. Usually, his mum and dad would be by his side for this whole experience. They would support him and talk him through everything.

Our dad would probably try and set him up with a nurse, or maybe even set himself up with a nurse, but he can't. One designated visitor for his whole time spent in hospital. Currently he's in intensive care after surgery and having broken 9 bones in his spine (literally top to bottom) and he's asking to be at home. The best our dad can do is facetime him at nights to try and keep him occupied.

Luckily for us we have an absolute boss of a dad in these situations, and nothing is too much. When you need him, he would literally drive to the end of the earth for you.

When you can say, I need help and they show up every time, sometimes as shit scared as you are, but by your side. He says he doesn't know where he would be without us, but boy are we lucky to have him.

I really hope I can grow up to be that person for my kids. They have been absolute troopers this year and have grown into their own selves. My eldest has developed his own sense of new independence from returning to school. He is beginning to learn who he is and has this polite and kind soul who occasionally lets loose a monster at home. In Fact, my youngest is very similar too, he is kind and caring. He acts as the medic and checks on anyone who's hurt, however when at home is also a monster. I count this as a compliment as this is their home and comfort zone where they can let loose. I will never have a pretty home, but it is certainly full of fun (and pee on the bathroom floor and leftover dinner on the kitchen walls).

Saviour?

So as of December 2020, almost a year after this shit show began, we are deeper than we have been before, as I'm led to believe anyway. More and more people are being tested meaning that our cases are obviously higher. Our death toll also now sits at 66,052 apparently. These are all people who have died that have also tested positive for covid-19. Not necessarily their causes of death.

However, our apparent saviour is here, the covid-19 vaccine is out and has been delivered to thousands already, mostly healthcare workers. It seems because nurses and doctors are our frontline workers, they are first to get the vaccine, however this unfortunately means they are first to rear the side effects. News is that a nurse is now in intensive care (the place she was trying to avoid) due to having this vaccine and multiple others had severe reactions and needed adrenaline to save their lives.

I don't know how I feel about the vaccine.
Which is fine. I don't need an opinion on everything really, especially if I don't plan to be actively involved in a solution.

Great expense

It's officially Christmas, well boxing day now. I've spent the past 2 months trying to enjoy and make the most of the season build up. It's been a year of not a lot so we knew Christmas would really take the biscuit.

Although everyone would want something like this to be extravagant, more people than ever are out of work and low on funds because of the state of this year. People aren't buying half as much because they can't, and more small businesses are going bust than ever. The worst part of all. The food banks are becoming like shopping centres and toy banks are being filled and emptied within days. People are becoming desperate. The bonus is community spirit is growing. Kind souls are emerging from the burning embers of broken towns to ensure no one goes without.

There are a lot of beautiful souls out there. There are also a lot of broken souls

Locked in

These past few weeks have been ridiculous, we were told that our area would be living in tier 3 until Christmas and then, would be allowed to have 5 days of festivities. Within tier 3 all non-essential shops must close, restaurants can only open until 6pm and no alcohol is allowed to be served, anywhere. This indicates that it's almost out of control, but it's ok to have a 5 day break at Christmas. Surprise surprise this quickly changed and there was only a break on Christmas day and the following day we would enter a lockdown of at least 3 weeks. I have an inclination it may be a few months again, but we shall see.

Another little kicker in the mix is a mutation of the virus which spreads 70% faster than the earlier strain. As with all viruses they mutate, however the scientists of the world are trying to decide whether it is more deadly or not, or weaker (or even the same virus at this rate).

And the kicker, this vaccine they have been pushing is possibly not going to be as effective on this strain that is spreading like fire.

All this crazy information is all true depending on which sources you believe. All of this could be an underreaction, or completely fake, really, I don't know anymore. Which governments and sources of any information can we trust? Who knows?

This year is ending, and it feels like it's trying to end me too. My hair has fallen out over the past few months worse than ever before. The urge to shave it all off is more than tempting, the only thing really stopping me is my partner. I don't know how well he would cope with me being bald. I do have a minor battle with myself to fight first, but that won't be a big challenge and I'll look like a lightbulb in no time.

I also realised I'm old and most definitely an adult. It hit me like a brick wall. Well not exactly a brick wall, but a rather large branch of a tree we were jumping on.

I went to the local woods with my kids and dog, just to enjoy my day off after a busy, grumpy week. The boys were climbing trees and jumping around in the mud, and I felt as if I had spent the day being grumpy and moaning at them. They started to hang on a branch and jump in it, so my idea of the day was that we all could jump on it, and it would snap.

As I started to stand on it, this little voice entered my head saying "this is cruel and is hurting the tree". How ridiculous the other side of my brain thought, and we carried on. I said to my youngest son to move to the other side as it would snap right where he was standing. He moved, it snapped and catapulted into my face. It smashed my eye with the most pain I have ever felt. I've given birth twice, but this was worse.

Luckily my eldest is pretty cool and calm and ensured we got home together, not the quickest we could, but he kept it all together. He got back to the house and made himself and his brother lunch. They ate it in the hallway so I could be with them while I cleaned my face up. A pretty large black eye and a headache for days but it's almost gone.

The green bruising currently sits there as a reminder of my own stupidity and ignoring those clever little inner voices.

The end of this year has left me with a strange feeling of being stagnant and happy. I am so very happy I get to be at home with my boys for that little bit longer. I get to hold them a little bit more and teach them. I kind of hope it doesn't end apart from getting to see my family. I relish nothing more than getting to spend time with them. My friends have also shown me this year that I'm not the only mad one and genuine friendships don't need to actually take that much effort. The love naturally flows, and right decisions are made when it's truly a respectful friendship.

For Christmas one of my friends knitted a massive blanket for me. I had no idea what to expect, but when I wrapped myself up, it felt like love. I received a few gifts that really genuinely felt like what I needed. I have gone from not having many friends I can trust to having more than I can keep track of. All from different walks of life with the same interest of no judgement.

Mum friends, work friends, school friends and help you through shit friends. Whatever friends you have, cherish them, and the weeds will work themselves away.

This year has taught me a few things, so it hasn't been wasted, in fact this year has far from been wasted. I have actually loved it. I will never get the chance to spend the amount of time alone with my kids as I did in 2020. (Well, 2021 lockdown so far is possibly showing that option again just to prove me wrong)

New Year, same shit

The only thing that has actually changed in the new year is the date. The virus is still lingering, and we still legally are not allowed to visit our families. That is except if you are in Australia. They have returned to living with hugs and venturing to wherever their heart desires. This is probably to be expected because the place is like the utopia of the earth and all you have to deal with is big ass spiders.

I have no idea what to do with my life anymore. I took a break from writing my daily musings as I was occupied elsewhere engraving glasses and helping my children embrace the excitement of Christmas. I now sit in limbo waiting to hear when I will be working and what actual work, I will be doing since my work cannot actually furlough me. Big bonus for me and I am very grateful for the boring life choices I made getting a stable and secure job, although it does feel like selling my soul at times.

The first lockdown of 2020 felt liberating, full of dreams, ideas and hope. This one feels like the opposite. Everyone's sick of being held captive and are doubting whether there's an actually genuinely good enough reason for it. I wonder if we applied our feelings to animals who consistently live in captivity for their lives, would the outcome be freedom. Or would we continue to convince ourselves that it was for their own safety?

#Harambe

Panic buying has begun again, and limits are being placed on particular items, particularly toilet roll and flour. I'm not sure what else as my ignorance has become a coping strategy to survive January.

My other coping strategy has included having a few groups of friends who are vital to my life. I have a best friend who I got to spend a few months of winter with, crafting and learning new skills, whilst taking the piss of her love life.

I have my 2 friends who live far away and have kids similar ages to mine. We spend the majority of time scheduling zoom meetings that we all cancel and doting over pictures of our broods.

I have 2 friends who live close but see them once a year at Christmas when they make a beautiful effort for my kids and whom I've been friends with for around 15 years. (Fuck that makes me feel old)

I then have a group of mum friends who all live nearby and have kids of similar ages to mine. We message every day and spend our lives being grateful to each other, listening to each other's moans and cheering each other up with ridiculous tik Tok videos.

Without any of these friendships I wouldn't feel whole. I wouldn't achieve half of what I have, and I would definitely feel like an alien without these likeminded people. They are true heroes in my life in their own individual ways.

I am trying my best to stay up and moving forward and I think I am doing well however my body disagrees. I've lost more hair this past year than ever before. One whole side of my head is bald, and the top of my head has a few patches of hair left that look like straggling weeds in a pond. I'm closer to shaving the whole lot off more than ever before and I'm still a little scared, but it's coming. I think it's been one of those things that from the start of losing my hair that I've been intrigued to do, almost like a bucket list quest. The only problem is that I may be stuck that way for good, which I'm far from ready for. If a charity was to spring up that I really wanted to raise money for then I would just go for it. (Kind of cheating because most of it is already gone.)

It will come.

My son has had a lot of mixed feelings towards me recently, I'm assuming because of the excitement of Christmas and not getting back to school or something to that effect. They usually happen in the evenings before bed, but the other night I lifted him back into bed, because he fell out. Being the kind mum that I am, I couldn't leave him on the floor.

He unfortunately didn't agree and did the only thing he could think of that would be mean, rolling over and sticking his tongue out at me. I was decked and literally couldn't stop laughing. I'm grateful it's all he really knows and luckily, he couldn't flip me the bird or suchlike.

It reminded me of rebelling when I was about his age. I wasn't a bad kid, but I did think I was the dog's bollocks when I called my mum a "bampot" whilst running through the house to hide. It was also never a question of whether to run or not, it was instinct because I did not want my ass to be leathered. If I was ever unlucky enough to be caught by my mum, she would skelp my arse and I would laugh, teasing "that wasnae sare" to which would invoke an even bigger wallop. I would love to say I only did this once, but I'm not the kind of person to learn a lesson like that so quickly.

Now the shoe is on the other foot. I don't know what to do in those situations and usually end up laughing, because legally I'm not allowed to hit my kids, no matter how much they entice me.

Tonight, I took off my living room door and cut a nice chunk off the bottom. I've had a new carpet for well over a year now and the door needed shaving, so it didn't drag. My partner insisted he would get someone to fix it ages ago and has never done, so I decided I was fed up waiting. It's far from perfect but I will see how long it takes for him to notice. Possibly another year.

The longest month of the year

So, the time has finally come, and I have removed the burden from my life of having hair. On Monday the 11th of January I gave up and shaved my head.

I say I gave up, but really this was the biggest battle I've had with myself. It took every ounce of strength from my soul to do and to say I was devastated would be a categorical understatement. I felt like I was taking away my femininity and what made me normal, but really, I was trying to rid myself of half a head of hair that was causing more distress than bearable. It felt freeing, but mostly gutting. I hit breaking point after most of the hair from the crown of my head fell out within the space of about 2 weeks. I blame the new year and the idea of entering a new adventure without any opportunity.

We entered 2021 with nothing to do but stay at home. It sounds great in theory but having some destination within the year would be nice. I don't mean a fancy holiday or even a shitty holiday, I just mean a challenge or idea of what new things we could learn or some way to move forward. Staying stagnant is worse than facing impossible challenges sometimes, I think.

I may regret ever saying that, but after a year of not being able to do very much and the possibility of another year of the same, it becomes a bit too constant. Also, its fucking freezing.

We can't even enjoy doing nothing in the sun because it's constantly minus 5, oh and you spend a fortune ensuring your home (that you are stuck in) is not at a similar temperature to the outdoors. I know this still feels like first world problems. Maybe that's also the problem, we spend so much time thriving that we forget what survival feels like and when it becomes that way of life we feel hard done to.

There was a strange night that led me to become like an uncle fester. I lay on my sofa at home the Friday before and could not control my heart rate. We had had a busy and amazing day out playing in the snow, but as evening creeped in, I couldn't feel relaxed no matter how little I did. My heart rate consistently sat at 108-110. My "smart" watch was telling me that I was doing a workout while my jiggly ass reminded me that I was perched in my usual spot on the sofa.

I made an agreement with my partner that I would call the doctor on Monday and then that night I would shave my head. I was really giving him time to adjust and be prepared for my baldness.

Looks mean something to him, no matter how much he pretends that everything's fine. This was more evident after I had removed my hair, however me being a bold ass warrior told him to sort his own shit out and come back to me when he could get behind me. It took him a few days, but he got there. He's a second child and has a habit of being dramatic. I do also love him to bits for it, however frustrating it can be at times.

Now the hard bit actually begins, I have removed the physical side of my panics (thanks to some nice wee beta blocker pills) and need to figure out why the fuck they are there in the first place.

I have a shitty feeling. Part of it comes from sitting on the fence for many years and watching good and bad things happen without actually having an opinion or action in them. I might be wrong, because that's kind of who I am (unless it really pisses me off, like looking at dish mountain! *)

Fuck this year already man.

*Dish mountain is the way my partner stacks dishes on the draining board. It always topples as soon as the washing machine is on, or you try and put anything away.

It's been a year

I gave up on myself largely in the past few months. This is my first time writing again this year and it's been almost 3 months. I spoke to one of my kids' teachers who reminded me of this covid diary and although the conversation was short and filled with random conversation from the kids, it reminded me that my blubbering writing was meaningful. Probably not to everyone but to at least someone it was worth reading.

I've spent a lot of time resenting myself and my own brain for having triggers and responses to anxiety. The sheer belief that my hair falling out was a sign of my mental weakness, where in fact it's just a reminder that I'm still alive and have emotions. Nothing so terrifying has happened that has made me stop wanting to live. I have so much to live for and do that having no hair shouldn't be the depth of my life.

This year my partner taught our 3 year old to ride his bike. No stabilisers just like that and he managed within a day. A feat that I wouldn't have attempted until at least later on this year and he was more than ready. He's my baby and so I spend a lot of time thinking he can't manage, where in fact he's stronger than I believe. Since then, he's just bloomed like a beautiful rainbow.

We've had a couple of brilliant falls, bumps and bruises this year also, including my youngest smashing the bridge of his nose off the edge of our garden path. Like a champ (or stubborn ass that he is) he refused a cold cloth or medicine and opted for some very large cuddles. My eldest also went flying off the front of a small toy digger landing upside down, legs in the air unable to get up. A small bump to his eye and some big hugs and he is also fine.

The constant falling and injuring themselves has helped soften the fear of losing the kids. They bounce back from the most ridiculous things and have been referred to as ninjas from onlooking parents. I take it as a huge compliment and just hope as they get older the ridiculousness of the stunts returns to a normal level.

I also tried CBT this year (cognitive behavioural therapy) with a local yoga instructor. She was absolutely fabulous and spent most of our meeting talking. Now usually that would drive me insane, however the 1 hour session was eye opening.

I basically gave her some small snippets of my life that stuck in my head, and she found patterns and triggers for anxiety inducing behaviour. At the end I got a final review of our session and some things to try when I feel myself losing it. I had high hopes and then became very quickly distracted by life, however I noticed that my heart began to slow easily, and I felt more comfortable within my own skin (even in its loose and jiggly state).

The power of someone genuinely listening and reorganising your thoughts is incredible. It's like hiring a cleaner for your mind. Instead of it being a disorganised mess, everything begins to naturally tidy itself away. Your scary thoughts don't disappear like ripping pages out of a book, however they sit in waiting ready to be organised at a time that you can catch up with it all.

Main lesson: give your body time to catch up with your brain. No one wants to participate if they always come 2nd place.

My body is far from a temple, more like a terraced council flat on the scheme, however it still needs love and respect, otherwise it will become a wasteland.

Big up to those people in life who take time to say: you're doing a good job, that was really hard, how has your life actually been?

You don't need to spend forever with someone to have a profound impact on their day.

I also owe a lot to my friends this year. I now have a group of people who are just as uniquely fucked up as I am. They are no pressure, no judgement, people who have your back in all the highs and lows. You don't need to be perfect, in fact you could be the shittiest version of yourself, and they are still there gearing you up to face another day.

With covid-19 we are almost back to where we were a year ago. Lockdown is still in place however restrictions are to be lifted shortly. Not everything but at least some form of normality will return. I'm not sure life will be as we have known it before. I have a feeling you are able to judge how well you trust someone by how close you stand to them. Still watching older clips of tv programs is bemusing. I watched a snippet of Gordon Ramsey in a restaurant talking to a chef (this time genuinely talking not getting ready to whack him) and he breathed on him.

Shocking, I know. He was encouraging the guy to take a few deep breaths before carrying on and I'm not sure what I found odder, someone being filmed so close to another human (who was not in his household) or the fact that Gordon himself was actually de-escalating a situation.

Either way it was ridiculously comical and shocking.

What will life be like in the new normal, who the hell knows.?

Video calls

So, life took a rather dramatic turn, and I did get back to writing daily musings, which became weekly and occasionally monthly. I decided to buy a website and publish my ridiculous stories online for a number of folks to read. It's lovely to hear snippets of others' lives as well as soon as I put myself out there. Life changed a lot and places began opening up and going out became normal again. It was a bit more exciting with a drop of fear thrown in.

More and more people signed up to get their vaccines and some ridiculous thoughts and ideas prevented me from ever receiving mine. As per usual an overwhelming thought about who would look after my kids if those vaccinated were segregated from the unvaccinated, halts me. I know it's probably a rather outrageous thought, but it seems in this day and age that ridiculous things have become the norm.

If I had said at the start of the pandemic that we would be locked in isolation for months and only allowed to go places if you were injected with an experimental vaccine, I would have been laughed at. However, this now being our reality is not such a confusing matter. It has been drip fed to people for so long that vaccinated and unvaccinated people are pitted against each other. It has just become another way to bully someone, which is all too common.

Anyway, these are only the rules in Scotland, and depending on who you talk to, depends on where you land up.

Unfortunately, this has become somewhat of a political war and on the streets, people are more aggressive and forceful than when we had the chance to vote on independence and Brexit. However, the repercussions of Brexit were swept under the carpet by the pandemic and an increasingly large number of people are encouraged to use private healthcare as waiting times have increased. Also trying to get past the receptionist at the doctors surgery is more like trying to complete an impossible level of the crystal maze.

If you are lucky enough to achieve this, then follows the waiting times and covid excuses as to why treatments are not available. Did I mention this is all done via video call, face-to-face is a whole new challenge?

Prescription sunshine

Anyway, there have been so many ups and downs, mostly confusing moments this year. So, I started CBT and then decided I would go to the sunbeds to try and encourage my hair to grow. I didn't continue the CBT which was probably my downfall, but because of the stability I felt after just a few sessions, I felt able to deal with life.

The fake sunshine was unreal, I called it my prescription sunshine. It worked so well in a number of different ways. I literally don't agree with the sunbeds usually and then I tried them. I got a boost of vitamin D (albeit minimally), my mood was lifted, my hair started to grow, and I felt like I was taking care of myself for a bit.

This lasted until I had used my 60 minutes up, which was my first top-up and then I just haven't gotten round to going back. They ran out in July and August is always such a busy month. It was also hot as hell! We Just spent a lot of time outdoors and it was fabulous.

By the time we reached July, I was still shaving my head smooth, because that's the way I had been most comfortable, however I quickly realised that I had a wedding to go to at the start of September that I didn't want to be bald for. So, I had to grow it out.

It wasn't fun and was a bit of a challenge not looking in the mirror so much or obsessing over it. Luckily, I have some really amazing people around me who want nothing more than success for me too. Everywhere I went I had a friend who was interested and anxious to see if I had given myself enough time to grow.

My outfit was organised by a multitude of offers from literally everywhere. I had my own personal Gok to help me at least find a style of outfit that would be suitable. I hadn't thought much about it until I looked in the mirror with one of my previous favourite outfits and saw how much more skin was on show. Not that the outfit didn't fit me, but my long hair used to cover my neck and shoulders (a part of my body I had previously ignored).

Anyway, thanks to some really amazing friends, I found something in a new style and was pleasantly surprised. Another friend also offered a flower crown which was ideal for removing the last of my insecurities.

Right up to the day of the wedding I still contemplated pulling out. I went to a friend who did my make-up for the day and decided that I wouldn't waste the time and effort she had put in so I must go. We went to the wedding and were swept away with how beautiful it was. The venue, the dress the whole day was fabulous and so was the company. We had a blast and saw some friends from forgotten years. It really was lovely.

After our meal and some brilliant speeches, I started to feel a bit off and put it down to the alcohol I had consumed, since I hadn't had a drink in about a year and half. At this point I also missed my kids irrevocably and was offered a lift home from another new parent, who was missing his baby girl. I jumped at the offer and felt like I had conquered my fear that had been consuming me for the past few months, with the added bonus of having a great time. Win win.

I was kind of on a high from the day, but still feeling horrendous, nothing in particular just feeling wiped. Definition of wiped; feeling like a soggy paper towel because I was useful for nothing, including wiping the floor.

Even at this point I was unaware of how crap life was about to get, I still had no idea I had Covid, or that my friends and family were about to be wiped with it too.

No symptoms until Sunday night. I had felt a bit off since Friday but was testing negative. It was just to be my luck that for the first weekend in a year that I actually had plans and was guaranteed to see hundreds of people, would be the time I would catch the dreaded Rona.

Of course, it still couldn't just be that I would be ill. This began a month-long downward spiral of what I can only describe as a succubus of darkness and pain. We were not the only ones caught in this despair. It literally sucked in my family and friends. There were challenges from every aspect of my life and none of them made life any easier or brighter.

My fears were becoming reality and the world quickly became an overwhelming bully. I ended up working a grand total of 6 hours in September. One shift. I had my 10 days of isolation to complete, (luckily it was no longer 2 weeks.) which I did and then was halted from returning to work for another day.

The day I was due to return, I was sucked back into the hole of isolation. A miscommunication from track and trace and some unforgiving phone consultants meant vaccine status ranked higher than common sense.

Unfortunately, this is still the case almost 6 months on. The only difference being the length of time you get trapped in isolation. This of course all hinges on negative semi accurate testing. (Semi accurate is being beyond generous.) This really did test all of my being.

Anyway, after my second dose of isolation was almost complete, I then couldn't return to work anyway. Instead, I got to spend the night by my gran`s side as we waited to hear news on whether my papa would survive or not. I wrote a journal log for that day just in case. I wanted him to know how much I adored him and the value he had always brought to my life. The ache I already felt at the thought of not having him with us. He was my hero, him and my gran always will be idols in my eyes.

I hadn't seen my papa since just before I had tested positive, and I was not to see him again.

The months blended together, and it was incredibly hard to accept normal life and reality. I hated the pandemic.

Now all this must be written in past tense, because it was literally 6 months ago. The length of time it has taken for my brain not to be complete and utter mush. For my memory to actually be present and allow me to write without a stutter. However even then it's taking a day of ignoring messages and human contact to focus enough to write.

Social exhaustion has become a thing now too. It's spreading fast and wide. We got locked away from people for so long, and then we were released. It was like a shark tank. Everything came to boiling point fast and now we know what peace looks like, the other end of the spectrum is beyond overwhelming. It is exhausting, which is also specifically annoying when you know so many nice and amazing people to talk to, but you physically can't connect the dots in your brain to maintain a conversation. I would settle for being able to talk normally without blurting out a vomiting version of hello, bye and hi: hibylo

How do I know I'm not the only one doing this: TikTok told me so? I am well aware this is not an accurate source for perception of reality, but if one other person in the world feels the same, then I'll take that. I'm not the only fanny, I promise.

The shit storm is nearly over, or so I hope anyway. It's done more than enough damage in so many more ways than I could ever have imagined.

Are you in or are you out?

Our current status in this country is beyond confusing. 1st and second vaccines were offered to end the pandemic, however now a booster vaccine is also offered, and the restrictions were altered to only allow freedom to those who had all three. Not what was promised or even suggested initially.
Unfortunately, the vaccine does not appear to stop you catching or spreading the illness, however it does allow you to get into a nightclub, as long as you can prove you have been jabbed.

None of it makes much sense, but there are plenty of distractions going on in the media for most people to ignore anything that directly affects them. All the famous pedos of the world are starting to be outed, Russia is having a go again at winding every country in the world up, taking submarines where they really shouldn't be for "training exercises". Can't wait to see how that situation will turn out.
The prince guy died, unsure of when, not the purple suit prince, the royal one (apologies, I just don't pay attention to know much more than this).

In England, you don't have to wear masks any longer and the isolation days are 5 days if you test negative. In Scotland it is still initially 10 days but if you test negative on day 6 and 7 then you can go free. If you test positive but your kids don't, they can still go to school until they test positive, as well as anyone in your household, as long as they have been triple jabbed.
Now there is more to the guidelines on isolating but as far as I can see each situation is dependent on who you talk to within the track and trace and really, it's just a minefield.

I read an article today about a man who had drowned and tested positive 23 times for covid. The need for testing a dead man? Don't know. Maybe once would be acceptable, however I really feel like they pushed the boat out with this one. Also, as we have said before, the world has gone mad.

I know I'm not the only one who is totally overwhelmed and confused with the madness and flying opinions that are being disguised as fact, so I have decided to do something about it. I spoke to the GP and told her I needed help to get rid of "Daisy", my overwhelming fear mate.

The Dr made it happen and then 4 months later I spoke to a psychologist. This was before the shitstorm that was September. So, by the time it came to a first appointment, I no longer knew what was the worst area of my life that I couldn't cope with. Really, it was getting ridiculous.

My recurring thought of that time was "stop the world, I want off".

It was odd, because I have an amazing support network around me, never once doubted that I was alone or the only one dealing with things, but yet still couldn't deal with society on a daily basis. Now to be clear, it never once affected my physical presence, actions or anything that was required for survival or blanketed existence in society. What it did mean though was that participating in interactions and trying to keep up, meant I was drained to the point of not being able to hold a conversation with those I felt comfortable with.

My mind felt like absolute mush and completing sentences without tripping over my own words felt like a mission to mars.

Finally, a win

Also, just had a moment of sheer delight, feeling like a fucking genius because I not only managed to revive my website, I made it beautiful and surprised myself. Celebrate it all.

Now to put this in a little more context: I had lost access to my website where I had written screeds and screeds of daily musings. I literally had no idea what to do and wanted to curl up into a ball of nothingness. I didn't however and I did what we all do facing the unknown... I asked to google, and it worked.

Alone

I have had a fabulous week again. When things just flow, not exactly smoothly, but no major catastrophes happen to us, and all is generally well. I can't say the same for the rest of the world because it has really gone to shit. The pandemic is almost over. I never actually thought I would get a chance to even hint at writing that without there being a major revolution within the government (which definitely should have happened either way).

Boris and his chums are avoiding facing their crimes against the people they are supposed to be serving and are trying to get into everyone's good books by removing all restrictions. The maddest thing they did was make the vaccine passport null and void.

So only a month ago, if you weren't vaccinated by the start of march, you were put out of a job. (Mostly for NHS workers and carers in England). I wonder where that stands now?

You don't need to wear a mask anymore or socially distance and the world is back to the grind of before. Problem is, no one is the same as they were before. People have dramatically changed, mental health has taken a nosedive and there are still some people who can't adapt so quickly to the ever changing rules. People were made to run scared and hide away from friends and family, to suddenly be told "just kidding, I changed my mind, as you were". They changed our way of living to be almost unrecognisable. We gave up so much and had a quieter life. You had no choice but to be with us and a lot of deep, dark scars were left. People were traumatised and you had no choice but to do it on your own.

All the situations we forget about being scary, without a hand to hold. Seeing your new baby on a screen for the first time, shouldn't have been alone. Those heart-breaking moments when mums saw those babies, only to be told they would never hold them in their arms. No one to hold or embrace the shock and devastation with.

The kids who started school and have never had a parents evening, school play or got to have a whole school assembly. The people starting new jobs, who never recognise their colleagues. Those that have been trapped in hospitals who died without seeing their loved ones, one last time. They held their own hand and their last words lost in the abyss. These people who never got to grieve a loved one, for fear over maximum numbers. The mums who birthed alone until the last minutes (if they were lucky) only to be left alone once again only hours later.

The kids who live in less than desirable homes, who were locked away for months, or who didn't have a decent meal for months because the schools were closed. The homes that were once filled with love and happiness then plundered into fear and poverty, because of job losses. The people who never saw their kids or loved ones for months because they were too scared to kill them by accident. The souls who dedicated their lockdowns to caring for others and risked it, without choice because that was all they could do. Sacrifices leave scars.

Reality is returning, but it is far too much for us to handle anymore.

Sanity? Where are you?

I am having a total out of body life at the minute. My presence is here but my mind has fucked off and went on holiday. Not even a good holiday, it has got lost along the way, ended up on the wrong slip road and has lost some baggage along the way, which of course will be sent back when it has returned.

This favours nothing in my life really apart from the desire to sleep, unfortunately it's only at the wrong time of day. I can't win, but really who in this life is winning all the time.

I honestly can't believe that I started my diary 2 years ago and the state of the world was a lot simpler than it is now coming out of this pandemic. It feels like we are at the end of one drama fest slowly crawling into another. It's impossible to keep up.

The world is like a season of Grey's Anatomy, the season where you don't know what's going on or who's going to die next and then suddenly all the cast are gone, and you don't know where to go from here. Strangely enough, I am doing similar things to what I did at the start of the pandemic and have bought my eldest another bike. The panic-buy bike from 2 years ago lasted approximately 6 months before breaking. However, it did serve a purpose and let a birthday wish come true.

This time we are hoping for a covid free birthday and less of the drama lama making an appearance. However, I can't help but imagine this next while being rather up and down. Even what feels like bright moments can flip turn and fuck you up.

I was watching random TikTok's with my sister the other night, having a jolly old time laughing our heads off until some kind person makes this video that would break a thousand hearts. It was a grandad in the video about to show his wife their latest grandchild, with the sound of "Bing bong" from Inside out (the Disney movie) in the background. The gist of the story was that he went looking for her and she was gone, to the heavens I imagine, and he was so sad looking for her. The soundtrack obviously intensified the grief and I lost it.

I howled my eyes out uncontrollably, and felt heart broken. Of course, the loss of my Papa is just still a bit raw. I don't know if it ever will not be, because really, he was just one of a kind. It just flipped my mood, and I took myself home for a long ass nap.

These long naps are what happens at bedtime, because you never get a full night's worth before one of the sleep thieves arrives, or kicks you awake. I believe by the time they are 18 we may finally get to know what a full 7 hours feels like. Wishful thinking possibly.

The time has grown closer to my eldest's now 7th birthday. We started the pandemic, and he was turning 5, getting ready to start school. We had no idea that this time, 2 years ago he wouldn't be returning to nursery, and we would all have an extended break hiding from the world.

If I knew then what I know now, I don't imagine my reaction being the same. We would never have stayed away from my Grandparents for any length of time knowing what the outcome of 2021 would have been. Luckily, we didn't waste too much time, but how I wish we had more time again.

I really brushed over the general details of the few horrible months at the end of 2021 when we lost my papa, but really it has been a protective reflex. The basic details were there, but the emotions of everything have been beyond description.

The worst of it all was the limitations that were put on us. Half of being stuck in isolation or trapped away from my papa while he was stolen away at the hospital. Putting our trust, faith and humanity in strangers to treat him with the love and respect he deserved and more. A soul too precious to us to expect any less. A death of a close loved one I don't imagine is ever easy

It's the end! (Just kidding)

We are almost officially at the end of the pandemic, masks are no longer law in Scotland and only a recommendation, and testing is advised if you have symptoms and feel unwell, but no longer required regularly. The virus has come to the final stage in its life cycle as it turns out.

I never knew this was how viruses work and are actually intelligent enough to evolve and change their strengths and effectiveness. Naturally a virus still exists but lives within society without killing its hosts so that it can survive. It's normal that it would come to an end, and we would just live with this virus like we do with everything else.

Whether this is the truth or not is up to your common reasoning to decide as all media sources are even less trustworthy than before (if that's even possible).

I am beyond exhausted this week. I managed to wipe myself out and get a bit of a chest infection, possibly because I was so tired and stressed that when I had annual leave from work, my body shat itself.

Unfortunately, I didn't get to rest it off much as it was my eldest's birthday once again and we had organised a birthday party. It was a great idea in theory, and we had planned so many things to do and all the kids he wanted to invite, (which turned out to be a whole 45 of them) but the day of the party was exhausting. I could have crawled into a corner and wept, but of course didn't and showed up for my boy. He was extremely grateful that on his actual birthday he let his little brother open most of his presents for him.

He has been beyond content and kind. Bat shit crazy at times too, but I believe that's part of him forever and I really couldn't ask for more from any of my boys. Without them, the past 2 years would have looked a lot different and quite possibly beyond bearable.

I still feel like junk almost a week later, so I will come back to this later. I just had to get my pride for them out there, so when they are grown, they know they have always been enough, even when they are mental. I love them both beyond words.

Rules? What rules?

Life has become so busy. Covid is pretty much a thing of the past, in fact when it's mentioned now people no longer quiver or even consider taking a few steps away.

I couldn't tell you about the rules for testing or self-isolation as I haven't been able to keep up for months now. It's June 2022 and finally it feels like the world is back to almost normal. Occasionally you do see the odd person with a mask on in shops and hand sanitiser still plagues every doorway, which isn't the worst idea in the world, people can be really gross.

People are venturing out all the time and workplaces are now filling up with budding customers. The only problem is that everywhere is still working with "covid staffing" meaning that the whole world is understaffed, and moaning is at an all-time high.

Companies trying to claw back the losses of the past 2 years are keeping staffing costs as low as possible and living in fear of another pandemic. So many businesses did not survive and those who did had to severely adapt. People changed their businesses to fit needs and made home delivery and outdoor access in as many ways as they could just to survive. Now that stuff is outdated, and people no longer need such pandering to and seem to have forgotten the local companies who bailed everyone out when we were all too scared to leave home.

These people became servants to the communities and now the world is picking up the good deeds that have been almost forgotten. As it turns out, every business is understaffed and filling the jobs isn't particularly easy. People have also found their worth and what makes life valuable.

When the world shut down, it was the connections we kept that kept up going, the humans that we kept in touch with. People found their real friends and where their love lay. To be paid minimum wage and asked to work like a dog is no longer enough. There's not an easy way to live comfortably.

You used to be able to study and work hard, go to uni and get a well-paying job. Those "well paying" jobs are not quite as desirable as you don't often end up much better off. You pay bigger bills and have more tax (unless of course you hit the super-rich bracket, then you are sorted) and the cost of everything has risen. To have a good job is not enough, so what is the point?

Trying to get a good job lands you in so much student debt it's almost impossible to be rid of and then if you want to buy a house you need to be extremely scrupulous with money. Skills that are often not taught to kids in school or at home.

Either way the system is a bit screwed and doesn't suit most of us, however, to change it is something I have no idea how to do as of yet. What I do know how to do is grow sunflowers and I have decided to create an army of them. I can't change the world, but I can make it a little brighter.
In fact, it may be a lot brighter. I have over 100 sunflowers sprouted and nowhere to put them yet, but I'll figure that out later.

I started writing this to preserve my sanity and got lost somewhere in the midst of it all. I lost my hair, my papa, my sanity and rather a few nights sleep. I did however ask for help and I got it. I got a community of people willing to help and listen, I had a GP who tried and a therapist who helped me realise what I needed in my life, and I got a shed load of memories and time with my kids and eventually the people I love.

This past 2 years has hopefully been a once in a lifetime opportunity and not a glimpse of what the future will hold. There have been so many great moments and times (something which we always know we are running out of), but it has been overcast with fear and tainted truths.

I still wouldn't take any of it back, but I don't think I want to do it again. My mission failed and my sanity is not intact, but I am content and for that I am grateful. I'm still bald and looking more and more like Harry Hill daily, but that I can also live with.

Where are we at now? My kids are now 7 and almost 5. My eldest has survived 2 years of school battling through a pandemic with no form of normal schooling. Isolation days for items that were brought home to be returned and segregation in year groups, only finally meeting the rest of the school this year. Extended holidays and so many unsaid goodbyes.

Time has been lost and the world is almost unrecognisable. Secrets of the rich and famous have been "exposed" and I use that term lightly as of course none of the haunting information of things that go on in dark corners is actually hitting mainstream media.

Our kids, in fact all of us are overexposed to information now and spend an extortionate amount of time being overwhelmed and run down beyond belief.

Although we got a break from the rest of the world in the pandemic, some of us have never been more involved in knowing more of what's going on beyond our doorstep.

People's mental health has suffered, so much to the point where asking for help isn't an option because the waiting list for services is months long and even when you get there, the services are still limited to what they can provide and more often than not, the problems that were real issues have become so long term people now believe that being anxious or depressed is just part of who they are now.

The price of everything has exploded. Petrol for example is £1.90 per litre. When I first began writing this it was £1.25. Our average weekly shop was around £40-£50, now we spend between £70-£90 and that could possibly be that we are splurging, but our eating habits haven't changed at all, but the shops we visit have so that it can stay slightly cheaper.

I wouldn't usually notice something like this too much, a gradual increase and all that but previously it wasn't necessary for both my partner and I to work, now however, I'm not sure we would survive too long if we didn't. I'm not sure, but the chase that used to be a career is pretty much over. We used to strive to have good jobs to earn a better wage and feel like we were successful. Now I limit my working hours to a set amount before I get blasted with tax.

They raised the minimum wage and gave us all a pay rise but did not change any of the tax brackets. Some families are worse off as they also raised the amount of tax they take from us, vetoing our pay rise. We pay extra for everything thanks to Brexit, oh and a new found excuse of the war in Ukraine with Russia. This topic also slips in and out the media depending on which MPs names are being brought up for their fraudulent activities.

Our kids don't know what normal lives are anymore and have spent a long time away from their peers, so have lost so many social skills. Anger issues in kids are beyond manageable and solutions are few and far between. Kids born in Lockdown are a whole new breed of untrusting, and the actual effects of the past few years will only become clear in many years to come. By this point I imagine the cause will be blamed on the war or petrol prices, or whatever they want to manipulate it to be.

There is great fear for the next generation and what obstacles they will have, knowing that life probably won't get any easier, it never has been easy, but the challenges they may face are unimaginable. I hope against it all, overexposure and constant battering of trauma gives the answers to the next lot of humans to make the world something a lot more pleasant than it is now. (On a global scale).

I couldn't imagine surviving this time being anywhere else in the world and not surrounded by the kind souls we have. We have had it easy in relative terms and for that I count my graces.

It really hasn't been all bad. In our home, I have never felt more secure and content. I can be myself and know what I like and don't. I have values that I know and have begun a new career because of this.

If I hadn't lost my hair, I would never have ended up seeking help and getting counselling. This in turn would have kept me living with "Daisy" in a constant daily battle.

Now I'm not saying I don't ever feel anxious and have been miraculously cured! (I am the messiah) However I do spend a lot less time worrying about my next car journey or staring at people wondering if they are about to have a heart attack. My kids have a lot more freedom and responsibility with their own fears, they don't have mine attached like an anchor halting them at every step.

They are allowed to be scared, they are allowed to be absolutely terrified, but we don't stop, we just have each other's back in those moments. They aren't alone. I am not alone. I'm fantastic and imaginative (hence the catastrophizing events) but I am content with that.

What have we learned? Not a lot.

Just kidding, life is short because it passes in an instant sometimes. It's still the longest thing we will ever experience, but holding onto the happy history is hard, because when they are gone, the grieving often makes us miss the good bits of the next moments and then they are gone too. It's hard to be like a sponge constantly and soak it all in without having to rinse out the bad.

Our kids need us more than we ever know. They don't need everything all of the time, but they need us to hold their hearts and protect them like the gold they are. It's not always easy joining in their chaos with our own charade going on in the background, but we are their teachers of all core beliefs and hold a strong power of their resilience.

We can't make all their decisions for them or protect them from every ounce of bad in the world, but we can sure as hell make them bad ass flubbers.

(If you don't know flubber it's worth looking the movie up)

My mind is still minced really, and none of this may make sense, but it's all good. I've had a good time making sense of my mince.
Let's hope it's not as plum to read.

Now a little catch up from the start. Did I miss moaning to my friends, no, because I still did it anyway on WhatsApp. Also, I had a lot less to moan about. I was a lot more content with the little things in life. The need to moan wasn't prevalent because I had breathing space. This didn't stop bad things happening, and it didn't help the way I dealt with my problems but moaning still didn't fix anything.

I ended up not dealing with my fears and anxiety, however this meant I was pushed even further into the depths of madness. Turns out a community around you and a busy life only staves away the anxiety (if you do it right anyway and play ignorance).

When the quiet comes and you have to face what's actually going on in your head, then it becomes a rather dark space. The thoughts creep even deeper and become less recognisable. You become a shell of the person you once were and if left long enough, this now becomes who you believe you are. You are not your problem, and you can't believe everything you think.

Now the actual phrase that was said to me was "not everything you think is true". It didn't even take a lot of comprehension to understand that my brain was possibly lying to me. It's amazing who you can't trust, even your own mind.

This week is now the summer holidays of 2022. It's been a mad year, but boy am I happy to have a break with the kids.

We are not planning anything exciting, but some time to build, make things and explore has begun! My gran has some of the best phrases and of course when we have spare time, we spend it with her and the rest of our family.

My army of sunflowers also became 300. Bit of a miscalculation on my part, but we are going to light up our little corner of the earth and do it again every year we can. There's already enough darkness.

Here's to the next pandemic!

George

For more utter nonsense and stories head to:
www.wearebigthinking.com

(If this website still exists by the time you read this)

Printed in Great Britain
by Amazon

85755918R00081